Digital CMO's Guide to Marketing Measurement

Think Like a Submariner For Operational Success

Bryan Semple
www.StoryMETRIX.com

overview of the entire measurement process. Part II focuses on the process of measuring and driving website traffic and converting it to sales leads. Part III focuses on measuring if a sales team is ready to follow up on leads, and the measurement of opportunity creation. Part IV looks at the people and processes required to make the measurement system work. Finally, Part V talks through the soft factors of philosophy and understanding what success looks like.

Special thanks to the marketing teams with whom I have had the pleasure to work at Trellix, Egenera, FairMarket (eBay), Onaro, NetApp, VKernel, Quest, and Dell. Interspersed with the sea stories throughout this book are anecdotes pulled from my years of experience as a marketer and marketing executive with these and other companies.

Also thanks to the Massachusetts Bay Transit Authority for providing a generally on-time, comfortable train ride from Framingham into Boston each day that allowed me 90 minutes of uninterrupted writing time on my way into the office.

Bryan Semple
Sudbury, MA

TABLE OF CONTENTS

PART I: Overview of the B2B Measurement Process

On your first pass through this book, this is a good section to read in detail as it sets the stage for the follow-on parts of the book.

- Chapter 1 explains how I leveraged much of my experience as a submarine officer to the task of measuring my marketing operations. There are many good parallels that will help a CMO understand the importance of measurement.
- Chapter 2 provides an overview of all the B2B measurement areas while Chapter 3 looks at the challenges to making these measurements.
- Chapter 3, the challenges, is especially important to understand. Most CEOs and CFOs believe that everything can be measured end-to-end since there are all these systems out there for measurement. There is some truth to this, and most everything can and should be measured, but such measurements may not live up to a CEO's expectations. It is critical that a CMO understand how to explain these differences.

Chapter 1: Think Like a Submariner

What You Will Learn

- Submariners measure everything to stay safe
- Submariners operate a predictable system
- Digital marketing is not as predictable
- Lack of digital predictability requires even more measurements than in submarine operations

Overview

Early in my career I had the honor to serve in the Navy on fast attack submarines. At the time, submarines were focused on intelligence gathering, strategic deterrence, and preparing to fight WWIII against the Soviets. To accomplish such missions, submariners had to operate fairly complex machinery in a hostile environment with a crew made up of personnel in their twenties. On the surface, marketing and being a submariner are not exactly similar. But as a new digital CMO at a purely inbound B2B-driven software company, the more I dug into the problem of building the operating framework for my marketing team, the more I found myself relying on the many lessons I learned as a submariner. This chapter walks through some of those concepts in an attempt to get a CMO into a submariner's frame of mind.

Submarines are Complex Systems

On a nuclear submarine, the core source of energy is a nuclear reactor. The reactor splits atoms and generates heat that is used to spin turbines, generate electricity, and turn the boat's propeller. The electricity from the steam the reactor creates is then used to power the weapons systems, ballast control systems, water-generation plants, oxygen generators, and air scrubbers via hundreds of different pieces of machinery. In case of a reactor shutdown, the boat relies on a giant battery to keep operating while it limps to the surface where a large diesel generator can be run to power a small portion of the total ship's load.

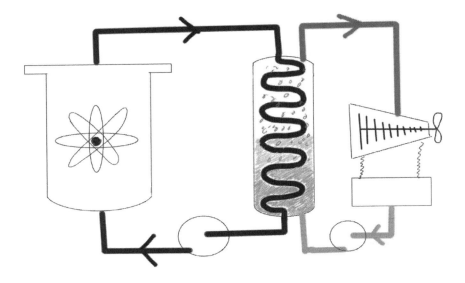

Figure 1: Fission creates heat that is transferred to high-pressure water. A steam generator acts as a heat exchanger and generates lower-pressure steam. Steam flows through turbines to create electricity and turn the screw.

All these systems have to be operated reliably and safely. A reactor plant shutdown caused by a safety system triggering means the plant stops generating steam. No steam means the ship's electrical turbines stop spinning. No steam means the screw stops spinning and the boat slows down. When a nuclear submarine deep under the ocean going more than 20 knots suffers a reactor shutdown, slows down, and gets heavy, it immediately starts draining its backup battery systems. Getting to the surface to stick up a snorkel pipe so the diesel generator can be run is critical. An under-the-ice reactor shutdown is even more problematic.

The net of all this? The officers in charge of the boat during any given six-hour operating watch must have a constant pulse on exactly what is happening throughout the ship. Depending on their assigned watch, one officer might be back in the engineering control room while another sits in the front control room driving the ship. But for every gauge in either control room, there are likely to be ten more out in the engineering spaces beyond the view of the officers in charge.

Gauges provide instantaneous readouts of various metrics, but issues in the submarine's operations are rarely instantaneous problems. Rather, they are often problems that build slowly due to gradual equipment failure or a series of cascading human errors.

Measurement: The Key to Safe Operations

When I was a submariner, we measured everything. At the time, we kept paper-based records called logs of many thousands of readings taken from gauges and meters and personal observations throughout the boat while underway and in port. Many of these readings were recorded hourly, others daily, and in extreme cases some were noted every 15 minutes. Readings could reflect anything from the temperature of the reactor core and the position of the reactor control rods to whether the machinery 2 lower-level bilge (a space on the boat) had any water in it. Some logs recorded the position of a valve. Other readings dealt with the status of nuclear weapons; the course, speed, and depth of the boat; the ship's position in longitude and latitude; atmospheric readings; or whether the topside sentry was alert while in port. The Navy had readings for everything. If even a minor incident occurred, we would take an additional log reading in order to prevent that issue from reoccurring.

While such log taking was important, reviews of the logs were just as important. Logs were reviewed and scrutinized not only by those recording the information, but also by their immediate supervisors. Supervisors had to make sure the records were taken in accordance with proper standards, and check to see if any emerging trends needed to be investigated. This review by supervisors also helped ensure everyone knew exactly what was happening in the ship during a given watch.

The knowledge level of operating metrics was not something that only the junior members of the ship's wardroom (i.e., officers) understood. Since the more senior officers of the ship had at one time been junior officers, they also knew exactly how the ship's systems operated in detail. A culture of questioning and understanding everything prevailed, and it wasn't abnormal to have the Captain challenge you on why something was behaving the way it was. For that matter, the newest seaman on the boat could also ask why something was behaving the way it was. For everyone to remain safe, this questioning was an important part of the culture.

Such obsessive behavior helps explain how the Naval Submarine Force was able to safely send boats to sea for months at a time, thousands of miles from home port, in extremely hostile environmental conditions, and have them return home safely.

Operating a Predictable System

For all the complexity in submarine operations, the system is actually fairly predictable. By the time I walked aboard my boat, the submarine service had more than 1,000 years of cumulative operating experience. My boat specifically was one of a nearly identical class of boats. The technology being used was tried and true and there were volumes of manuals describing how to do everything. Since we were dealing with well-known and documented engineering concepts, the boat's operation was predictable.

The reactor, for example, went critical at predictable rod heights since we knew how many hours of total time were on the reactor and we knew how fast the cores burned out. We could predictably adjust rod heights to bring reactor coolant temperature up to the right band. We knew the impact that opening the throttles would have on coolant temperature, and how many turns it took to open the steam valves to get the turbines spinning at the right speed.

Yet, even with all these known responses to inputs into the system, we were ever vigilant for the one-in-a-million sequence of events that could lead to our demise at one extreme, or simply leave us operationally impaired at the other. But it was never the obvious errors that got a submarine into trouble. Much of the obvious points of failure had been engineered out of the systems and processes over the previous decades of operations. The trouble points occurred over a sequence of mishaps caused by human error or mechanical failures in a combination that the operators did not detect. Identifying and overcoming such trouble points required vigilance, measurement, and a questioning attitude. It was critical to make sure systems were behaving in a predictable manner based on the settings and inputs to the controls.

Digital Marketing Measurement is Complex

Measuring the effectiveness of digital marketing is simpler in some ways than measuring the effectiveness of submarine operations. The technology behind the operations is not as complex. In general, operators of digital marketing equipment are using cloud-based systems to analyze data and work with this data through point-and-click interfaces. There are very few physical interactions or systems. A laptop and a browser are the key tools for operations. Submarine operations require a massive variety of physical systems that deal with very real pressures, temperatures, and voltages as well as toxic and radiological chemicals. This is done in a hostile environment as the boat is surrounded by sea pressure that could crush it. Submariners might have to don an air mask in seconds to fight a fire and know how to put on and take off anti-contamination clothing. Meanwhile, marketers simply sit in their comfortable cubes in business-casual clothing and click away.

But digital marketers operate a system with many more unknowns than a submariner. Digital marketers are attempting to influence highly unpredictable humans through a remote, online process. Unlike submariners, who work within a tried-and-true military system, digital marketers are constantly trying new, unproven strategies and systems to improve yields in an ever-changing landscape of communication. Twitter was not on anyone's radar five years ago. Facebook was not a medium for B2B lead generation three years ago. And each online marketing operation is built out of a unique collection of content, systems, offers to prospects, and the specific attributes of a single industry. When companies are in the same industry selling similar products to similar customers, this generally defines them as competitors, which makes the sharing of information impractical. Meanwhile, most subs are part of a nearly identical class of ships within which, for the most part, benchmarks and readings can be easily compared between boats.

Digital Marketing is Less Predictable than Nuclear Fission

While online marketers operate in a slightly less complex environment than submariners, they also operate in a much more subjective and less predictable environment than submariners. For the submariner, Uranium-235 plus sufficient neutrons going at the right speed create nuclear fission and generate heat in a highly predictable manner. Add enough ballast to a trim tank, and you can predict how that would make a boat sink or rise. Push the stern planes down 10 degrees at a particular speed, and the change in the ship's angle would also be predictable.

B2B marketers operate in a much more unpredictable world. Rather than try to manipulate highly ordered neutrons, B2B marketers attempt to influence and communicate with human beings. Most aspects of such interactions, from the perspectives of people visiting a website to their reactions to the various offers and content and colors on the site, are highly variable. Even the demographic of the people visiting a website are somewhat out of the B2B marketer's control. A blog posting by a high-traffic blog could drive massive traffic to a site that is a surprise to the marketing team. Conversely, seemingly random changes to Google search engine algorithms could dramatically change traffic patterns for no apparent reason. For the submariner, such dramatic changes would be equivalent to waking up to discover the salinity and buoyancy of the ocean had changed overnight and the buoyancy characteristics of the submarine were no longer valid.

Submariners are always concerned about a series of events or failures that could lead to problems on a boat. Here is one area in which submarine and web operations are similar. Most submariners don't worry about a sudden catastrophic failure that would lead to their demise. All the major design flaws have been engineered out of the boat over the preceding generations of ship design. Websites are similar in that they are now up 99% or more of the time. Website content on B2B sites is generally organized along the same lines, making it easy for prospects to find the information they need. Forms are standardized and operate in a uniform manner. Pay-per-click measurement systems are fairly sophisticated, showing the ads and keywords that work along with lost impression share due to budget and poor ad quality. Real-time site monitoring and analytics can instantly show the status of a website while also showing the exact path a visitor is taking through a website. CRM systems like Salesforce.com can track leads and contacts as they are turned into opportunities while also bringing in real-time clickstream data for individual contacts.

Taken as a whole, it is easy to sit back and say, "My website is up, people are visiting, my pay-per-click programs are working, I can see leads going to sales, and I can see sales generating opportunities. All is well." This will generally be the case for nearly all B2B operations. But these are the table stakes to operating a site.

Without a culture of continuous measurement and investigation, this false sense of satisfaction can actually mask problems and a disastrous marketing effort. While a website may be up 99% of the time, response rates may be so slow that most visitors rarely venture into the site. Forms may be standardized, but if abandonment rates are high, no one is submitting the forms. Just one 404 error can cripple the site experience for many users. Search engine robots can be unknowingly blocked from key pages. Pay-per-click traffic, while converting, may be originating from suspicious sites located outside of geographies that even have sales coverage. Leads provided to the sales team could be sitting untouched. Opportunity generation may be occurring, but it could be coming from direct traffic to the website rather than any of the spending from marketing programs.

Without ongoing, careful, and in-depth monitoring of the entire lead process and site operations on an hourly, daily, weekly, and monthly basis, significant problems can creep into marketing programs without tripping obvious alerts to senior management that something is wrong. On a more elemental level, without ongoing, careful, and in-depth monitoring, it is very difficult for the marketing leadership to actually understand what is even driving their marketing operations.

For B2B marketers today, there is no cookbook, no reactor plant manual, no standard operating procedure on how to succeed. Technologies are shifting too rapidly, the systems contain too much data, the volumes are too high, and the experience levels of those on the teams are too low. The best a B2B marketer can strive for is to create a culture of constant measurement so as each new change comes along, as each experiment is undertaken, as the market shifts beneath one's feet, new tactics can be attempted, measured, and evaluated. There is no other way to accomplish this without building a metrics-oriented organization that is constantly revising, changing, and questioning B2B marketing operations.

The following chapters will use this submariner-B2B marketer analogy to walk you through which types of metrics should be tracked and analyzed and, most importantly, how to build a metrics-oriented organization.

Take Action
- Document your current flow from website visitor to deal.
- Inventory the current measurements you take. Are all parts of the process monitored?
- What is your confidence level that all website forms are operating, all lead routing rules are working, all sales reps are following up on all leads on any given day?

Chapter 2: Overview of B2B Measurement Areas

What You Will Learn

- Overview of the B2B marketing and sales process
- The different types of website traffic
- How to measure the website conversion process
- Measuring opportunity creation effectiveness
- The nurture process
- Measuring sales effectiveness

Overview

In Chapter 1, we discussed the need to measure everything in B2B digital marketing. While B2B marketing does not involve the very high risk level of submarine operations, the philosophy of measuring "everything" still applies. Modern marketing systems may measure almost everything and make it easy to analyze data. The challenge lies in figuring out which measurements to use in order to effectively drive a positive marketing outcome. Open up Google Analytics or Webmaster Tools or Salesforce.com and you'll get enough metrics and numbers and reports on your website to make your head spin. In this chapter, we will walk through a broad outline of these measurement areas.

In general, digital marketers need to:

- Drive traffic or visitors to a website
- Get these visitors to say "I am interested in your solutions"
- Help educate these prospects so they say "Can I talk to sales?"
- Empower the sales team to add value to the prospect discussion so prospects become customers

To accomplish these four steps, six general areas of measurement are employed:

- **Website Traffic or Visitors** – Without traffic, there are no leads
- **Website Conversions or Responses** – The percentage of visitors to the website that either a) complete forms and convert from anonymous

website visitors to responses or b) complete some type of goal that can be measured

- **Nurture Measurements** – The amount and success of response nurturing that attempts to create sales-ready leads
- **Lead Conversions** – The percentage of responses who, over time, convert to sales-ready leads
- **Opportunity Conversions** – The percentage of sales-ready leads that, over time, become sales opportunities by entering the sales funnel
- **Deal Conversions** – The percentage of sales opportunities that, over time, close and come out the bottom of the funnel

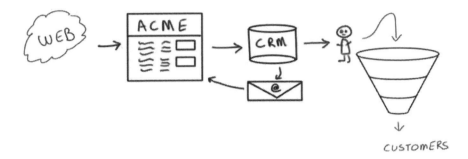

Figure 2: Traffic goes to a website, where it is converted to responses. Some of these become leads, others are nurtured. The sales team takes some of the leads and put them into the sales funnel.

There are other measurement areas such as data quality, process quality, and website health that also require measurement, but these are not as core as measuring the flow of prospects through the selling process. In addition, there are detailed measurement areas for each of the above steps. Pay-per-click (PPC) advertising, for example, has its own set of measurements that detail the cost and effectiveness of advertising. As we develop the model, we will explore these areas in greater detail. In addition, there are other programs that do not drive website traffic, such as pay-per-lead (PPL) programs offered by many media companies. In such cases, the conversion from anonymous browser to sales prospect occurs off-site, but the balance of the sales cycle and measurement occur within the control of your company.

The measurements above track a repetitive process of driving traffic, converting on the website to a prospect, nurturing to a sales-ready lead, converting to an opportunity, and closing the deal. Over and over and over again, 365 days a year.

Of course your B2B model could be different than finding people, engaging them, and closing opportunities. You might also have a strategy that does not use a corporate website but exists entirely on a social community platform. Whatever process you use to engage and close prospects, it is critical that you divide it up into individual process steps and determine how to measure each section. Without this, you are running blind when trying to make decisions to improve marketing effectiveness.

Let's look at each of these areas in detail.

Finding Prospects and Driving Traffic

Finding prospects and getting them to a website is the first part of B2B digital marketing and the first area of measurement. While online is one way to connect, these same prospects also congregate at conferences, trade shows, and user groups. The "old school" physical events strategy must not be overlooked. But measuring traffic online is the first key step in the digital marketing process.

Since not all traffic is alike, the concept of traffic segmentation is critical to measurement. There are numerous great resources online for understanding the segmentation imperative. Avinash Kaushik, one of the top analytics people in the field and the digital marketing evangelist at Google, has published numerous posts about segmentation on his popular blog Occam's Razor at www.kaushik.net.

In broad terms, there are two types of traffic: organic traffic that a company receives through its market presence, and paid traffic that costs a company money. Website traffic needs to be placed in segments since it behaves differently on your website depending on the source. Think of it this way: If you were at a trade show, people might come by your booth because:

- They are looking for you (organic - direct traffic)
- Someone at the show told them to go check out your booth (organic - referring site traffic)
- They saw an ad for you in the program (paid traffic)
- They see a word on your booth's graphics that seems to match a problem they are trying to solve (organic - search traffic)

Each of these types of booth visitors will react differently when they come to your booth. The direct traffic people will walk in and say hello. The referring site people may be more cautious, while the people who saw the advertisement may hang back and try to figure out who you are. The online world is no different. Keep in mind this useful analogy to the physical trade show as you read on about new ways to approach online marketing.

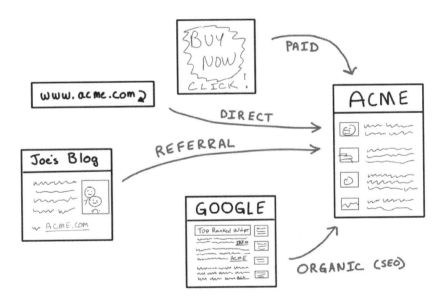

Figure 3: Website traffic should be divided into component parts.

Understanding Organic Traffic

The best type of website traffic is "free" or organic. Free is in quotes since nothing is ever free, and in fact getting free traffic takes significant work and effort. But organic traffic does not happen on a pay-per-visit basis so, despite the work and effort involved, its costs are several orders of magnitude less than the costs of paid traffic. Organic traffic also keeps coming long after efforts have stopped to build it. Unlike paid traffic, which can quickly stop when an advertiser literally turns off your ads, organic traffic is based upon much more resilient links and rankings and brand awareness elements that are remembered by prospective sales leads. The impact of such links, rankings, and brand awareness fades slowly, even after efforts to build up your company's marketing presence from a certain angle are stopped.

While looking at organic traffic as a whole is good, more segmentation is required. Organic traffic can be divided into direct traffic, search engine traffic, referring site traffic, and email marketing traffic. Each of these areas can be further subdivided on its own.

Direct Traffic

Direct traffic is comprised of visitors who simply show up on your website by typing in your URL. It can be very difficult to determine the intention of these users as you have no trail that might indicate what led them to your site. Other forms of arriving traffic are likely to be accompanied by information that includes a referring URL or perhaps the marketing code for the email program that was used to send a message. Where direct traffic lands on your site does provide some clue about visitors' intentions. Consistent direct traffic to the careers page of a website, for example, indicates that a collection of people looking for jobs at your company have bookmarked your job site. In general, however, much of a site's direct traffic reveals little information about visitor intention.

Search engine traffic is another source of organic traffic. Organic search engine traffic occurs when someone types a query into a search engine and selects one of the links that come up in the search results. Two types of results appear from such a search. Paid search results usually show up on the right side of a browser or at the top of the results. These are not organic search results, however, and we will cover that next. The organic results are the results beneath the paid advertising where the search engine has amassed the best list of links it believes matches the submitted query. Your link's position on this page, the text that is displayed from your website describing the link, and the number of times people globally search on these terms all impact the amount of organic search engine traffic that shows up on your site.

When traffic from a search engine arrives on your site, it carries with it the search term used in the original search query. If your site sells tractors and prospects arrive at it via searches for "Front Loaders", this information is captured by your site's analytics package when such visitors land on your site. Such search term indicators can tell you what people are searching for, but also what Google finds relevant about your site.

Search terms that result in traffic to your site can be divided into branded and unbranded keyword searches. An unbranded search is a generic search keyword that does not contain any of your company's brand names. A branded search term might contain your company name or a product name.

While all search traffic is welcome, unbranded search traffic is especially important since it usually includes visitors who would not normally look for your site online, but came across it as part of a broader solution search.

"The Good, the Bad and the Ugly"

A blog posting my company once did entitled "The good the bad and the ugly" on IT management was suddenly very popular and continued to be popular weeks after it was published. It wasn't until we reviewed our keyword referrals that we realized we were picking up traffic from people searching on "The Ugly" from the title of the original Clint Eastwood movie "The Good, the Bad and the Ugly". Unfortunately, the intersection of Clint Eastwood fans and people interested in our product was very low and the bounce rate for the blog was nearly 100%.

Referring Sites

Referring site traffic is another source for finding prospective leads organically. In this case, other sites create links that take people to your site. An article on CNN.com, for example, that talks about your company or products and includes a link that takes people to your site is one example of a source for referring site traffic. Referring site traffic is tough to come by since it is essentially impossible to control whether or not people write about you and link to your site. It is extremely valuable, however. A single solid product review on an influential blog with a large amount of traffic can drive high-quality referring site traffic for many months or even years. Of course the opposite is also true. A poor product review can drive traffic, but perhaps not the kind of traffic you want. Referring site traffic can come from classic press sites, influential blogs, blog comments, community postings, video sharing sites, and social media sites such as Twitter and Facebook. This listing is growing yearly as different types of content sites emerge that could be relevant to a B2B marketer.

Measuring referring site traffic in aggregate is important but, like search engine traffic that contains the keyword of the search term used in the prospect's search query, referring site traffic also contains the actual URL where the referring site link is located. So not only, as in the CNN case above, could you tell that traffic was coming from CNN, you might be able to tell on exactly which page of CNN's site a reference to your company was made. This can be invaluable intelligence to have as it allows you to determine what threads and topics people are discussing that not only warranted a mention of your company, but resulted in valuable referring site traffic.

The overly simplistic key for improving search engine, direct, and referring site traffic is to publish great content; build market-leading products; and create a following that other websites, bloggers, and social media heavyweights will mention and hopefully link to. Such creation of inbound traffic is a highly valuable specialty in which companies like HubSpot, Inc. are experts.

Email Marketing Traffic

The final piece of organic traffic is email marketing traffic. While some will disagree that email marketing traffic is organic, let's put it in this category for simplicity's sake. Email marketing traffic to a website results from emails sent by a company to addresses listed in its prospect database. Keeping this traffic stream separate from others is important since, theoretically, this traffic is highly qualified. The prospects are also already known, so this traffic will behave differently when striking the company's website. Email marketing traffic usually hits a site with tracking cookies, so theoretically it is also easy to identify.

Understanding Paid Traffic

Paid traffic is the second major method for finding B2B prospects. While organic traffic is free, it rarely results in enough traffic and enough leads. Paid traffic helps to fill in this gap. Today's paid traffic can also show up as direct or email marketing traffic tomorrow as more and more people get to know a company and its website. Paid traffic can also add value as it provides a way to expand a prospect database and reach out to prospects who have perhaps dropped from nurturing or other programs or have never engaged in your sales process.

Search Engine Ads

Paid Google advertising is the most prevalent form of paid traffic. In the paid search model, advertisements are displayed on the search results page that a search engine returns after a query. In addition to Google, Yahoo and MSN offer similar capabilities. Advertisers pay each time someone clicks on one of these ads (hence the name "performance-based" advertising). Clicking on an ad takes the prospect to the advertiser's website, where it is up to the advertiser to more fully engage the prospect.

In this advertising model, advertisers bid for page position. The higher the page position, in general, the higher the number of clicks to the advertiser's site. Of course the expense is also higher for the more valuable positions. From the search engine perspective, algorithms seek to maximize revenue for the search engine through a combination of displaying ads that are clicked frequently and ads that carry a high bid. For this reason, being the highest bidder doesn't necessarily guarantee an increase in your site traffic, as Google is not going to waste its highest-performing ad positions on ads that are not likely to be clicked and don't make them any money.

Advertising Networks

A slight variation on search engine advertising is called ad network advertising. In this situation, relevant ads are displayed on multiple websites that are part of the advertising network. Unlike search engine advertising, which only appears on search engine results pages, an advertising network displays ads on websites throughout the internet, providing a much greater inventory of pages for advertisers. A website operator of a popular blog can join an ad network and receive advertising revenue from the network operator each time someone clicks on an ad that is displayed on their site. All it takes to join is simply some HTML code and an account with the network operator.

In this model, there is no search box to provide a clue to the type of ad that could be of interest to the prospect. Instead, ads are displayed based on the content that is displayed on the site. Once the site operator joins the advertising network, the ad network crawls the site and determines applicable ads based on found content.

For a given 24-hour period, significantly more web pages are served up on these advertising network sites compared to the search engine results pages on Google or other search engines. In other words, significantly more ad inventory is found off Google.com than on Google.com. For this reason, advertising networks can provide the vast majority of advertising opportunities for companies. However, since the advertising is contextual to the site, and the site operator is incented to display a broad array of ads to see what sticks, click-through rates and quality of clicks are usually low. These networks also have the potential to dramatically drain budget dollars and bring low-quality traffic to an advertiser's website.

Bad Incentives

A contractor was hired by my department to drive a pay-per-click program. The goal was to get trial software download costs below $60 per ad. There was also an unofficial arrangement that if this succeeded, the contractor would get a bonus. The contractor achieved exactly what he set out to do; his efforts quickly resulted in incredibly high numbers of downloads at about $60 per ad. Because we had no robust measurement system in place, we thought this was good, until we overheard the sales team on calls to some of these leads.

Upon further investigation, we realized the contractor had employed all kinds of shady tactics, from placing misleading ads saying everything was free, to paying no attention to the quality of the sites on which he was placing our ads. The result was poor-quality high traffic that downloaded our trial software for free and did nothing else. We cancelled the contract with the firm, brought the program in-house, and never looked back. We made our share of mistakes, but what we ultimately delivered was of such high quality that, to our surprise, we actually maxed out our spending on Google for traffic.

Pay-Per-Impression Advertising

In addition to search engine and ad network advertising, banner advertising and sponsored blog sites represent another form of paid traffic. In such cases, the business model is slightly different. The term banner advertising generally refers to the business model in which advertisers simply buy a number of impressions for their ads without any guarantee for clicks to the website. This cost-per-million impressions model was the original advertising model on the web and is still available on some sites.

For smaller sites that may lack the ability or desire to run impression-based programs, a simple sponsorship model may be used. In the sponsorship model, blog sponsorship ads are displayed for a set period of time rather than a set number of impressions. For sites with low traffic or sites that don't want to reveal traffic numbers, such a simple sponsorship model provides a way to gain advertising revenue.

Physical Events

Online is not the only place to find people. In some B2B verticals, potential prospects attend robust trade shows and events on a regular basis. Far more than just branding events (depending on the concentration of potential prospects as a proportion of total show attendees), these events can be gold mines for finding customers. With an online B2B model, however, ultimately these people need to get online and come through the website to learn more. B2B sales are generally complex and require additional white paper information, product information, and potentially even product support information. When the selling model involves partners, these resellers or distributors also are mainly reached through the website. So while tracking the number of attendee badges swiped at a trade show may be a good starting point as well as a point of interest, measuring ultimate online engagement of such attendees will reveal how far down the sales cycle many of these prospects ultimately travel.

Watching daily and weekly traffic numbers by source is extremely beneficial. Without this knowledge, leadership can set incorrect expectations around key marketing events. A product launch, for example, sounds like a big deal. For some mega-brand companies like Apple, a launch drives mega traffic. But if you are selling into a niche space, product launches may not be that exciting. The latest model of a 4-ton front loader, for example, while very exciting for a tractor company, may not be that exciting for the public at large. So understanding relative volumes of traffic from sources is critical. My department knew, for example, what a mention in an online trade magazine would drive. We also knew how much a top blogger could generally drive with a mention of our products in his blog. With this back-of-the-envelope information, it became easy to prioritize our efforts. The answers were not always obvious, however. The core press that our PR team spent so much time courting was terrible at driving traffic compared to what appeared to be obscure blogging sites.

The same holds true for paid traffic. With level spending, paid traffic numbers will change, but not dramatically. Email blasts, if they are done the same day of the week each week, will start to drive repeatable traffic. If such efforts are done correctly, a team will fall into a rhythm of knowing how much traffic will show up on the company site on a given day based on what is happening in the market and the day of the week. That is the sign of a well-engaged team.

Measuring Website Goal Attainment

Measuring traffic to a website from all sources is the first key aspect of measuring digital effectiveness. Depending on a traffic source, there may be additional information and data available. For example, in the case of paid traffic, clearly understanding the cost of traffic is important. For search engine traffic, keyword information may be present. This is all good data to analyze, and we will discuss this aspect of the process in later chapters. But once traffic gets to your site, what are the goals?

For many B2B sites, the main goal is to advance a prospect down the sales cycle. Before you can set a goal to advance someone through your sales cycle, however, sales and marketing need to agree on exactly what steps the buyer goes through, from initial awareness of the company to becoming a customer. An understanding of these steps can then result in the assignment of certain behavioral actions to each step. Comparing these behavioral actions to actual prospect behavior then provides a yardstick to help your team assign a prospect a spot in the buying cycle. Different spots in the cycle should warrant different sales and marketing responses. For example, if it is determined that a prospect who hits the "Request a Quote" button is ready to buy, having a sales response that involves a call to the prospect and provides an overview of the company is probably not appropriate. It is critical to develop the buying cycle so a series of behaviors can be postulated that indicate where a prospect is located in the cycle. And it is critical to respond to those behaviors in an appropriate way.

Defining the B2B Buy Cycle

Many books and articles and blog posts have been written on how to define a B2B sales cycle. A highly generalized buying cycle might contain the following steps:

- **General Awareness** – The prospect is aware of your company
- **Solutions Awareness** – The prospect is aware of the solutions your company offers
- **Solutions Research** – The prospect has a pain and is searching for a solution
- **Technical Evaluation** – The prospect is ready to get a short list of vendors and do some type of detailed evaluation to see if any vendor's products meet the prospect's needs
- **Business Justification** – The prospect has selected a product or products and is completing a business justification or total-cost-of-ownership

analysis
- **Purchase Decision** – The prospect selects one product for purchase and works through the purchasing process
- **Close** – The prospect is now a customer

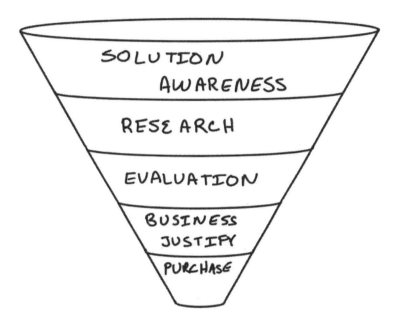

Figure 4: The B2B sales cycle needs to be defined so a best guess can be made as to a prospect's location within it.

Some companies get very detailed on the process steps, while others might stick with a more broad outline. Consulting and other firms will have their own variations on the process. Despite differences in nomenclatures, certain steps need to be defined. For example, some companies only start a formal sales cycle map when leads are given to the sales department. However, in a B2B digital selling environment, this would be a mistake since prospects can self-educate and take themselves far down the selling cycle without even contacting a sales rep. Hence the concept of a sales cycle is actually dated, and should be looked at instead as a sales and marketing cycle to reflect the full process, from awareness to a closed deal.

Digital marketing, especially at high volumes, means a prospect may never need to talk to a sales rep to become a customer. Theoretically, with enough information and prospect enablement on a company's site, purchase orders should just roll in. (If only it were that easy!) Still, the sales and marketing cycle must be defined with the understanding that sales "qualifying" a prospect may never happen.

Measuring Prospect Location on the Sales Cycle

Most prospects don't self-identify where they are on the sales cycle. In fact, even if you ask a prospect where they are in the buying process, they typically don't know. A prospect could believe they are in the technical evaluation phase since they are evaluating a product, but in fact they are really in solutions research. Perhaps the prospect is a Purchasing agent and has yet to talk with a manager about the scope of the problem the company is trying to solve. In such a case the prospect has jumped to evaluating products without first getting full agreement around criteria.

Top sales reps know how to tease out the information from prospects and accurately assess where they are on the buying cycle. For a marketer, however, there is unlikely to be much, if any, conversation with prospects. Rather, marketers have to rely on behavioral clues expressed through website clicks to make a prediction of where someone sits in the cycle. For each sales cycle stage, below are some possible clues:

- **General Awareness** – Anonymous website traffic
- **Solutions Awareness** – Attends a general webinar, seminar, or event
- **Solutions Research** – Reads solution part of the website
- **Technical Evaluation** – Downloads product white papers and technical briefs
- **Business Justification** – Looks at pricing pages and downloads case

studies

- **Purchase Decision** – New visitors to the website show up and don't register, indicating potentially that purchasing agents are looking at the company's products
- **Close** – The prospect is now a customer

With agreement on the online behavior exhibited for each of the buying steps, a marketing team can now construct goals for the site.

Creating Goals

At this point, the marketer has traffic coming to the site and an agreed-upon behavioral profile for the different sales cycle steps. Now the key is to translate these profiles into goals that can be measured on the website. In the simplest format, if the sales and marketing team agree that anyone who clicks "Send Me a Quote" on the website is in purchase decision mode and agree that these prospects should go direct to sales, then a goal for the website could be to generate the maximum number of "Send Me a Quote" actions on the site every day. This is certainly a worthy goal, if only it were that easy.

If the marketing group could generate the required volume of these leads every day, the sales team could be a very low-cost organization focused on order fulfillment. Most complex B2B selling processes, however, operate at nowhere near this level of simplicity. In fact, it is usually the opposite, with sales wanting and needing to be engaged early in the process, usually at the solutions research phase, so they can start to shape the conversation and the evaluation criteria a prospect will use to select products. After all, each competitor's sales team is also trying to shape the selection criteria to their company's advantage.

There is another problem with the extreme example of having only a single goal for the site based around the number of people who hit the "Send Me a Quote" button. Most website visitors are not ready to be sent a quote. In fact, the vast majority are nowhere near that stage. So to measure success on this extreme measure would lead to under-reporting the success of the site in engaging prospects in the sales cycle. The key is to set goals that can represent multiple sales cycle steps in order to give a true picture of how effective the site is at moving traffic or visitors through the various goals within the sales process.

Example goal types could be:

- Signs up for a demonstration
- Downloads a datasheet
- Watches a video to the end
- Has high page counts in the product information section
- Completes a form for a topical datasheet
- Looks at pricing
- Completes the "Contact Sales" form

For some marketers, the attainment of site goals may be disconnected slightly from sales cycle steps. A prospect hitting the "Send Me a Quote" button is most likely in the purchase decision stage and can be assigned to sales. But a prospect downloading a white paper could be anywhere in the process. In some cases, the completion of a single goal may not map cleanly to a stage in the sales cycle. In this case, it could be the accumulation of goal completions within a period of time that is used to determine sales cycle location. This type of system, called a lead scoring system, involves the use of a collection of site activities and goal completions to determine a best guess at sales cycle location for a prospect. We will discuss the actual scoring aspect of this system in later chapters.

Measure Goal Conversions

Loosely speaking, hitting a goal is sometimes called a conversion. Measuring goal conversion rates is important as you strive to understand the success of a website at both attracting the right type of traffic and converting that traffic to the next level of the sales cycle. Conversions take all different forms.

In some cases, a goal conversion is attained when anonymous traffic is converted to a named prospect through the use of a form. In another case, a goal conversion could be reached when someone downloads a white paper in response to an email. In the latter case, the marketing automation system may already know the downloader since the prospect has clicked on an email with a tracking code embedded in it that corresponds to contact information in the marketing database.

Conversions may identify potential prospects that don't have a need for the company's product today, but could in the future. While not valuable for sales today, building the database of potential prospects for nurture marketing is critical to long-term success. Conversely, conversions may also identify those prospects with acute pain that are far down the buying cycle and ready to purchase. Whatever the reason for conversions, the key is to measure them by traffic source and conversion type.

Tracking conversions by traffic source is key. Direct traffic to a website theoretically should convert at a higher percentage rate than pay-per-click traffic. Why? Direct traffic is comprised of people who know your company name and URL and, for whatever reason, are coming straight to the site to do something. PPC traffic, on the other hand, may result from prospects' split-second decisions to come to the website based on an ad they saw while conducting searches on Google. The ad may or may not correlate directly with the search, though hopefully it does, and the offer you present such prospects may or may not match what they are looking for. Think back to the physical trade show example. If I come to your trade show booth directly because I am looking for you, the chance of me converting through a goal is much higher than someone who sees an ad in the show book and wanders by wondering "What do they do?"

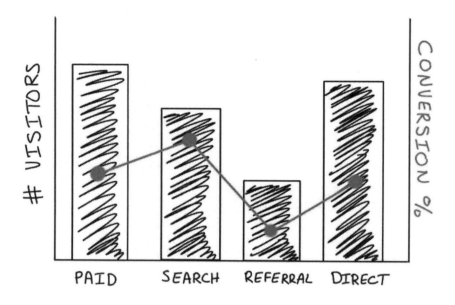

Figure 5: Traffic needs to be measured both by segment and the conversion rate by segment.

Of course, like all things in digital marketing, the statements above may not always be true. If your company announces it has just been acquired or if some other general news about you reaches an audience beyond your prospect base, you could see a significant amount of direct traffic or even referring site traffic that arrives but doesn't convert to a goal. A good example would be if your company is featured as a "Best Place to Work" in a local publication's survey. Direct and referring site traffic may soar as job seekers arrive at your site and then divert to the careers section. In such a case, overall site conversions for the site could go down for the week. A CMO not paying attention to the details of what is happening on the site could incorrectly conclude that the prior week was disastrous when in fact it wasn't. The week simply represented a surge in traffic not from prospects, but from job seekers.

A similar example with different results can be shown with PPC traffic. Pay-per-click traffic is very finicky and can be manipulated. A PPC ad with the words "FREE" in it running wild on ad networks can drive mega traffic to a website. If the landing page where this traffic hits requires only an email address to get this "FREE" item, then site conversions will spike, traffic will spike, and the CMO will look like a hero. Until, that is, sales starts following up on the leads, or the remarketing effort starts. In this case, the data quality of the people may be found to be so far off, even if they match the prospect profile, that the program is deemed a waste.

The same goes for social media tracking. A sudden increase in people liking your company's Facebook page is almost always a good thing. But if their "Likes" are driven more by their desire to enter a drawing you're running on your page, the quality of their "Likes" is much less than that of a potential prospect who likes your page simply because, well, they like your company. Not all Facebook "Likes" are the same, just as not all conversions are the same.

Let's go back to our trade show booth for another example. Companies spend millions on trade show trinkets. Some marketing teams obsess over the giveaway at their company's booth. They hand out tee-shirts, for example, then measure the success of the show based on the names collected by handing out tee-shirts. Name collection is certainly not a bad thing. But which has more value to your sales department, a collection of names of people who grabbed a free tee-shirt, or a collection of names who spent 10 or more minutes with a sales engineer looking at the product, but walked away with nothing? Tee-shirt names represent low-quality, high-volume traffic. Sales engineer engagement names, however, are high-quality, low-volume names. The hurdle required to meet a goal is drastically different in both of these cases.

Not only, then, does the quality of traffic need to be considered, but the hurdle required for a prospect to reach a conversion goal is also critical to understanding overall goal conversion rates. The hurdles that can be put in front of a prospect to reach a goal could include:

- Number of pages viewed in a single session
- Length and number of required fields on a form
- Length of video required to watch
- Attending versus just registering for a webinar

- Amount of time spent talking to someone at a trade show
- Registering a downloadable software product
- Providing an accurate phone number in a form field

Conversion rates without context to what was required to convert are generally meaningless. Marketing team members who spout off stats like "We got 3,000 leads from the trade show" without qualifying that number by saying "by giving away tee-shirts" are distorting conversion results. Online team members that say "25% of our visitors from pay-per-click download trial versions of the software" without adding "we only require an email address and we advertise the software as free everywhere" are distorting what is actually happening. In both of these scenarios, the statistics carry no meaning when presented without context.

Itchy Skin in the Battery Well

The beauty of all this marketing measurement is that the data is usually just a point and click away. All the measurements can generally be accessed in real time in the cloud. Even physical trade show events have wired their badge scanners into a network so real-time badge scans can sometimes be grabbed. This type of measurement is easy and you don't have to get your hands dirty to do it. Such ease of access to data was not the case on the boat when I was in the Navy. Whether I was walking around the engineering plant taking paper logs or watching endless gauges, I did everything manually. Little information was presented in electronic form in the 1980s.

One of the worst places to have to take measurements was the battery well. The sub's battery was a massive lead-acid battery about the size of a living room with its individual cells standing about three feet tall. The battery was a collection of cells wired together and jammed into the "well".

The battery was a critical component of the ship's operation. If the sub were to suffer a reactor shutdown at depth, steam would almost immediately stop being produced, tripping off all the electrical turbines. The ship's propeller would also stop spinning. Being at depth and suddenly losing power is not a good experience for any submariner. If a boat is trimmed out heavy, loss of speed would cause it to slowly sink. Since the boat is underwater, there would also be no air available to run the diesel generator.

Through a combination of coasting to the surface and quickly restarting the reactor and the battery, a boat in such a situation would remain safe. The battery would take over, providing electricity to critical loads while the reactor is restarted. Obviously it was very important to correctly maintain a ship's battery.

For maintenance, you had to climb into the well and crawl across the top of the cells to take measurements. You had to crawl because there was no more than 1-2 feet of clearance between the top of the cells and the overhead. To enter the well, you first had to remove all metal from your clothes lest you get between two terminals and close the circuit through the metal on your body. Since the battery contained acid, you also had to wear a uniform that would gradually get destroyed by acid.

To take measurements, you would crawl into the well with a partner and slither on your stomach to find specific battery cells for sampling. Cells would be measured and refilled if necessary and the measurements of the cells specific gravity would be recorded. It was critical to make sure the battery was healthy since a battery fire was a particularly nasty fire to fight on board. Sampling the battery was not an easy way to get data. Marketers rejoice: You don't even have to leave your office chair to get your data.

Opportunity Creation Effectiveness

With traffic coming to your company's site, a known sales process defined, and conversion rates getting measured, the next key item to measure is the opportunity conversion rate. Opportunity conversion represents the point in the sales cycles when a sales rep is ready to acknowledge that an opportunity exists to sell a product to a prospect. Criteria for opportunity creation vary from company to company and sales process to sales process. Some companies require a prospect to have pain, a budget, and some kind of compelling event to make the transaction happen. Other companies may have lower or even more stringent criteria. Then, of course, there are the sales reps. New reps tend to create lots of opportunities when they initially start selling due to their optimistic view of the sales process. More experienced reps tend to be more conservative about opportunity creation because they have learned that the over-creation of pipeline does not endear them to management.

Opportunity creation is different than forecasting. Sales forecasting is the commitment to sales management that a deal will close within a certain time frame. Opportunity creation is simply adding opportunity to the sales pipeline for the sales rep and making the opportunity public for a manager to see. The downside for the sales rep: If the deal goes away, it has to be marked in the "lost" or other type of loss category. The upside for the sales rep: Active opportunity creation usually results in less management pressure.

Regardless of the dynamics that surround opportunity creation at your company, understanding the rate at which leads passed to sales result in opportunity creation is an important component of tracking marketing effectiveness. It is one thing, for example, if Google AdWords converts traffic from an anonymous browser to someone who downloads a white paper and provides a marketer with their name. It's another thing, however, to determine whether this person is a valuable prospect or just a student looking for information on a topic.

AdWords will only measure the conversion that this person provided their contact information and completed a form and hit a thank you page. Sources like Twitter will only tell you that someone is now following you. YouTube will alert you to more followers. The litmus test for these followers, clicks, and form completions ultimately lies in the answer to this question: Do they convert to opportunities? In the long term, you must track back to each program or source so it can be credited with contributing to — or not contributing to — opportunity creation. Without this check and balance, false-positive conversion rates will drive marketing resource expenditure on programs that convert browsers to names, but do not convert to actual opportunities.

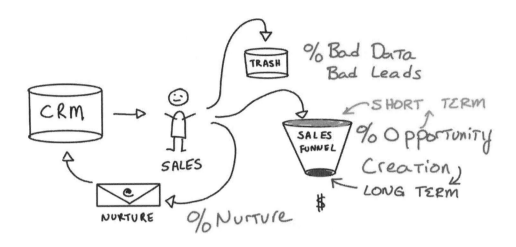

Figure 6: Short-term opportunity creation measures the initial sales rep lead disposition and entry into the funnel. Long-term opportunity creation measures what comes out the bottom of the funnel.

Some teams will want to track all the way to opportunities closed and will seek to assign a specific marketing program to a closed deal. This will get discussed in later chapters, but given the complexity of B2B selling, trying to find the one program that drove a sale is unlikely. It is like trying to provide a sales team with the "one thing to say" that will get a prospect to buy. B2B selling involves a collection of interactions. Trying to point to a single specific interaction or program is not an accurate way to assess results.

The other challenge inherent in looking at closed deals as the measure for marketing programs is the delay that closed-deal measurement can introduce in marketing program effectiveness tracking. A closed deal may take months, even years, to happen. A marketing program can't be left to run without feedback on opportunity creation rates for months. This feedback needs to start coming in within days, or at most weeks, of the program's kick-off.

While tracking opportunity creation rates for a lead is important, tracking other possible end states for a lead can provide equally valuable marketing and sales information. The vast majority of leads passed to sales will not result in opportunities. Of the prospect names passed to sales, some will have bad data and be unreachable. Others won't be prospects even though they exhibited prospect behavior. Other leads will be prospects, but without a compelling reason to purchase. Still others will not respond to a sales rep contacting them. Tracking this disposition information is critical in order to spot ineffective sales follow-up on the rep level and also to track broader trends in lead programs.

From a lead program standpoint, a program that generates a high percentage of leads with bad data (or leads that are not even prospects) should be cause for concern to the marketing team. Conversely, over the course of several programs, a rep who is consistently below average for opportunity creation compared to peers on the same marketing programs should also be of concern to the sales team. Tracking lead disposition is critical for evaluating marketing and sales effectiveness.

Nurture Measurement

When prospects passed to sales do not generate opportunities, these leads need to be nurtured. This is an entirely separate and unique area to measure. The reality is that a vast majority of B2B prospects will not convert initially and will end up in the nurture cycle. Nurture cycles generally involve email marketing on a recurring basis. Nurturing involves staying in front of prospects with value-added information and content so when they are ready to enter a purchasing cycle, your company's name is top of mind.

Of course nurturing can also involve members of the sales team or a more junior lead development team proactively reaching out to the nurture database. This type of prospecting into the database is almost mandatory if you look at the typically low open rates of emails and the click-through rates of online advertising. Ideally, marketing should be able to locate opportunities that arise from the nurture database. Yet there is no substitute for direct prospecting, especially into prospects that meet the target profile and potentially have the pain, even if timing of the first contact impeded opportunity creation.

Nurturing effectiveness is measured by counting the number of prospects in each stage of the sales and marketing process and tracking the names' movements in aggregate. Numbers of active prospects should continue to increase each month as more and more names are added to the database. A portion of the names being nurtured will eventually go inactive and drop from the database. Other names will eventually activate and be sent to sales, while others may sit in a limbo state in which they engage, but only casually, for some time. The key is to understand the movements of prospects in this stage and to feel comfortable that nurturing programs are improving your yields of sales-ready leads.

Measuring Sales Effectiveness

Once prospects are determined to be sales ready, sales can spring into action. There are two broad measures for sales. The first is their response time to new leads and the second is how prepared they are to respond to these leads. Following up on a white paper inquiry within minutes does no good if the sales rep doesn't understand the domain area well enough to add value to a prospect in a phone or email conversation. Conversely, if the best trained and most educated sales rep takes a month to call a prospect from a trade show booth, it is unlikely the rep will be successful. For such reasons it is critical to measure not only how responsive members of a sales team are, but how prepared they are to respond effectively to leads.

Measuring sales rep response time starts with establishing requirements for responding to inquiries and leads. As is true with many topics covered in this book, the subject of timing and methods for following up on inbound leads is one that numerous experts have explored and discussed in detail. Regardless of the sales philosophy or program your company implements, it is critical to understand how to effectively measure that response times have been met. A simple rule stating that all leads from marketing are followed up within 24 hours with a phone call and within seven days with an email presents one example of simple and easy-to-track follow-up criteria. Without this criteria established, and without measuring it, there is little likelihood that a sales team will follow a consistent process for engaging new sales leads. Without this consistent engagement process, measuring lead disposition results, including opportunity creation, gets exceedingly difficult since all the leads do not experience the exact same rep follow-up process.

The second half of effective sales measurement is to measure how well the sales team is trained to sell the company's products. Measuring sales effectiveness can be done across two dimensions: training and the availability of field enablement materials.

For training, completion of sales training courses, grades from these courses, and attendance at weekly sales training updates all measure knowledge transfer to the sales team. These areas can be broken down based on completion percentages, average grades, and attendance scores to create an aggregate number for training performance. Field enablement materials include items such as competitive kill sheets, Microsoft PowerPoint overview presentations, and technical white papers. The completeness and current status of such core sales support materials should be measured. Developing a matrix of required sales enablement materials is the starting point for measuring the effectiveness of field enablement.

Figure 7: For sales effectiveness, sales reps need access to resource library, training, and process compliance

Cruise to Nowhere

Just like a sales team needs to be trained, the crew of a boat is almost always training. In addition to training on their areas of specific responsibility, the crew as a whole has to train on certain boat-wide tasks. These tasks could include firefighting, damage control, getting underway from a port, repelling boarders, or loading supplies for several months underway. To get a boat ready for sea, the pinnacle of training preparations involves the "fast cruise".

The fast cruise is nowhere near fast. In fact, you go nowhere. For several days, all the crew members come aboard the boat and simulate going to sea. The gangplank is pulled, crew members simulate getting underway, people go below decks, hatches are shut, reactors are set at critical, air is recirculated. Except the boat remains next to dock. You may even be able to see your car, but you are locked on the boat for two or three days.

While sales preps needn't be as intense, measuring the effectiveness of sales training is important to see how well prepared the sales crew is to catch and follow up on leads from marketing.

Measuring Customer Success

Many books have been written on how to measure customer success. We won't attempt to replicate this knowledge here. Yet it's important to note that the final piece of measuring the marketing chain is to measure customer success. From a digital marketing standpoint, there are ways to determine customer happiness and engagement. These methods including measuring engagement with customer nurturing programs, customer traffic to the website, attendance at webinars, traffic to customer communities, or the number of customers registered and participating in the community. These measures simply scratch the surface of customer success measurement, but are nonetheless good indications of customer engagement.

Take Action

Measuring B2B marketing effectiveness requires a focus on website traffic, goal attainment, nurture monitoring, sales rep effectiveness, and opportunity creation. While theoretically these steps sound simple, we will see in the next chapter that there are many obstacles to implementing them all into an effective measurement program. Understanding these obstacles is critical to surmounting them.

In the meantime, familiarizing yourself with the basic drivers mentioned in this chapter is a good start:

- Log into Google Analytics for your site to see the different traffic sources.
- Determine what goals are already configured in Google Analytics.
- How is the sales cycle defined at your company? How is it implemented in the CRM (customer relationship management) system?
- What defines a lead for the sales team? What are the opportunity creation rates for leads? What are the opportunity close rates?
- How do you know if the sales team has been properly trained?
- What type of ongoing training programs does the company use?
- Download the metrics summary sheet that is a companion to this book www.storymetrix.com/resources and review the overall sections.

Chapter 3: Obstacles to Effective Measurement

What You Will Learn

- The reality of the B2B selling process – it is complex, and tough to track
- Data sets don't align to make what appear to be simple questions, like the ROI on a program, have easy answers
- Low traffic volumes and response rates can be statistically insignificant when evaluating programs
- The difference between causation and correlation and why you have to be on guard for this with your team
- Dashboards can make you stupid, not smarter
- New selling technologies make the problem set more complex to solve
- Methods to rise above these challenges

Overview

In the last chapter, we walked through the high level areas of measurement for B2B marketing. Various vendors of marketing automation systems often make measuring this effectiveness sound simple enough. Certainly marketing and sales automation systems are a piece of the solution. But for total visibility there is no single system, spreadsheet, or person in a sophisticated B2B operation that holds the answer. This chapter will review some of the challenges that arise during the measurement process.

Complex Selling Processes

By its nature, a B2B selling process is complex. The products tend to be complicated, expensive, and designed to solve difficult problems. From a customer perspective, multiple people tend to be involved in the selection and purchasing process. While a technical buyer may evaluate a product, the business buyer, the person who can write the check, is usually someone completely different. Various recommenders and influencers may be present in the process in addition to internal politics that may shape which vendor is ultimately selected. The process itself may take several weeks to several months to even a year or more, depending on when marketing began nurturing the prospects and how rapidly the sales cycle completes.

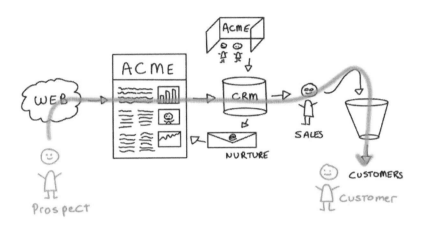

Figure 8: The unrealistic B2B sales process

Since the process itself is complex and takes place over an extended period of time with an extended list of players, it is reasonable to assume that multiple marketing programs will come into play throughout the extended sales cycle. A prospect may initially learn of a company through a friend on Facebook. This could lead to an anonymous online visit, followed by a serendipitous physical meeting at an industry trade show. The prospect could then go dormant completely, and re-engage months later based on an article he read on his favorite blog. The article could prompt him to type in the company URL, visit the company website, then — within a single online session — grab a white paper, read the blog, and leave the site. Sixty minutes later, the prospect may decide to return to the site but, this time, the prospect types in the company name into the search bar, clicks the branded Google pay-per-click ad that is present, arrives back at the site, then grabs another marketing asset. Of course between the first anonymous visit and the prospect's re-engagement, the prospect may clear his cookies, erasing any previous online trail. This scenario is not as far-fetched as it may sound. Reviewing web records and campaign records in a marketing automation system for closed deals will often reveal this type of twisted, roundabout path to a deal.

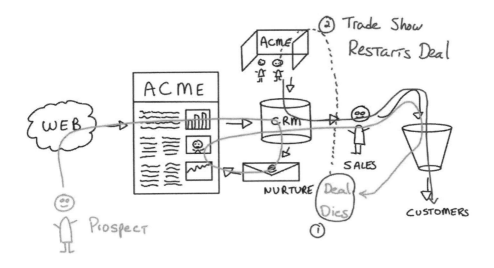

Figure9: The more realistic B2B process with multiple actors, multiple stop/starts, multiple programs.

The complexity of the process means that there is no easy answer or measurement point that provides end-to-end visibility for program effectiveness. Nor is there a single system that holds the answer. This is heresy to many marketers who want to assign specific ROI metrics and deal-closed metrics to specific marketing programs. It is also heresy to the various dashboard, marketing analytics, and CRM vendors. But any simple answer would, to at least some extent, ignore the complexity of the B2B selling effort.

Marketing efforts can be measured and must be measured. But such measurements involve a combination of art and science.

The complexity of the sales cycle is the first major challenge inherent in the measurement process. The different data sets required for analysis represent the second major challenge faced by marketers.

Different Data Sets

The variety of data sets available for B2B marketers is both a strength and a weakness of effective measurement. The sheer numbers of databases and the amount of information they contain — and the relatively cheap cost of obtaining and analyzing this information — is staggering. Data warehouses for marketing analytics used to be a preserve of only the largest companies. Now, with cloud-based service models, any company can access and analyze mounds of data that could unlock the secrets of their prospects' and customers' behaviors.

Most marketing teams use a variety of systems to support the entire marketing and sales pipeline. Web analytics systems look at clickstream data. Search engine optimization systems mine keyword data while also analyzing page rankings and the HTML code on a website. CRM systems organize names in hierarchical accounts and contacts structure for sales rep manipulation while also tracking opportunity creation and deal closure. Marketing automation systems track marketing campaigns, programs, and response rates. Content management systems organize pages and display content out of databases. Cloud services like YouTube or communities like LinkedIn provide usage data on views, visitors, and followers. Webmaster-oriented tools provide data on page errors and crawler statistics. Phone systems provide sales rep dialing statistics while phone home systems may provide data on actual product usage.

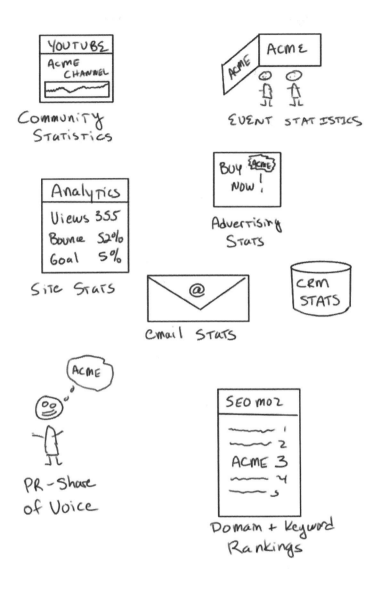

Figure 10: Marketers have access to multiple data stores and applications.

All of this information, if analyzed correctly, can provide insights into the health and effectiveness of your company's B2B marketing efforts. But the variety of information types is great. Unlike someone analyzing a financial system that deals in a unit of dollars, you are striving to understand a system that consists of marketing clicks, conversions, traffic, leads, talk time, etc., all varied units of measurement that must somehow be tied together.

In addition, even the analysis process is more complex than that of a financial system. Money doesn't just flow in or out of a marketing system. Traffic comes in, changes shape to leads which then go to a sales rep, and those leads can go through any number of additional steps from there. There is no set defined path. In fact, almost every interaction is different. Yet the effectiveness of each individual interaction must be measured to determine what is working and what is not.

What starts as content-driven and ad-driven metrics shifts to clickstream data, shifts to contact information, shifts to opportunity tracking, then hopefully ends up as a closed deal. The differences in data structures are staggering, but yet these differences have to somehow be knitted together in a logical fashion to determine which of the early-stage programs most impacted the later-stage opportunities.

When organizations attempt to link programs together from stage one of the sales cycle to stage five, they invariably get themselves into trouble. The linkage is too far and there are too many other factors that impact opportunity creation. The key is to determine how to measure the effectiveness at each stage of the sales cycle with the disparate data sets in such a manner that marketing resource decisions can be made. This has to be done without jumping to the conclusion that all of this can be conclusively linked into one analysis from one system that can somehow provide the answer. Of course every year new companies are formed to provide the latest in dashboards or analytics to do just that. As we will discuss later, to some extent this is not a technology issue. It is a management issue. The trouble comes when the CEO wants to understand the opportunity pipeline from the number of "Likes" the company's Facebook page has received. The correct answer is that the impact of Facebook "Likes" is tough to determine. But if you can establish that traffic from Facebook to the company's website keeps going up month over month, that your "Like" count is increasing along with it, and that Facebook traffic converts, then it would be safe to conclude that getting more "Likes" is a good thing. Of course by the time you read this book someone may have figured out how to track "Likes" to leads, but today that is not the case. And tomorrow, there will be a new digital technology that will be just as poorly understood.

In the same way attempting to link multiple data silos together to determine if a Facebook "Like" drove an opportunity is dangerous, it is just as dangerous to only perform analysis at one part of the process. Examining the number of sales-ready leads and the programs from which they originated as the only measurement that matters provides such a narrow piece of the analysis puzzle to almost be meaningless. For each of these lead sources, what was the opportunity creation rate? For each lead source, how much did it cost to generate the lead? How much traffic was required and what were the conversion rates for each source? How are these rates trending? Each part of the process needs to be measured and tracked for the total picture of what is happening to ultimately emerge.

Business Process Challenges

Digital marketers have access to many systems for analysis. Yet even these systems that theoretically are designed to provide easy answers to questions are impacted by their own structure, the business logic that is implemented, and the fact that humans are doing data entry and making process flow decisions.

Take, for example, the concept of attaching product information to a customer record. Are products sold to individuals or accounts? If they are sold to individuals, are they attached to the individual who originally clicked on, for example, the pay-per-click ad, or are they attached to the final buyer, the purchasing person, or perhaps even the ongoing support contact? Perhaps products are attached to the account name only. Either way, such a variety of possible distinctions makes it very difficult to connect the pay-per-click ad John Smith viewed to his company that ultimately may have purchased the specific product mentioned in the ad.

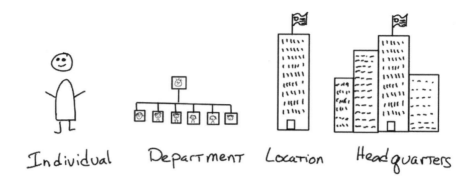

Individual   Department   Location   Headquarters

Figure 11: How do you define a customer?

Traffic Measurements Can be Complex

Something as simple as measuring online traffic is actually not as simple as it appears. Segmentation of traffic is critical to understanding website behavior. But accurately separating traffic based on segments relies on the strength of the analytics package used and of the traffic to carry with it clues as to its origin. User behavior can also distort traffic measurements. Is a user who types the company name into a search box direct traffic, search engine traffic, or just a lazy typist?

The challenge is that, for a variety of reasons, out-of-the-box analytics systems rarely get it right when segmenting traffic. Traffic generated by email marketing can many times appear as direct traffic depending on the device being used to read the email. Pay-per-click traffic doesn't always show up in the algorithms as paid traffic. Paid traffic from smaller niche advertising networks that the analytics package doesn't recognize may show up as referring site traffic. With new browser capabilities, someone who typed your company name into an address bar may actually have been conducting a search, a fact that distorts whether the visitor was actually direct traffic or a search engine result. Many free analytics applications also use only a sample of total site traffic, further distorting results.

Correctly classifying traffic actually requires knowing how to run the analytics system and understanding about the types of domains that would send traffic to a site. It is not uncommon, for example, to see significant traffic from a news website and to falsely conclude that news about the company must be driving traffic to the website. With greater scrutiny at the source URL and landing pages, a trained eye can determine that the traffic was actually coming from a pay-per-impression banner ad program that was displaying the company's ad on relevant pages. Only by getting into the details of traffic can organizations really determine what their true traffic sources are.

Strange Traffic from Area 51

We witnessed a sudden increase in our paid traffic coming to the site. To accurately track all paid traffic, we used the word "/paid/" in all paid traffic landing pages. In addition, paid traffic would also theoretically have click IDs since most of it came from a formal advertising program. The sudden increase in traffic was noteworthy, since it was clearly paid Google AdWords traffic with AdWords click IDs. The traffic, however, appeared to be going to pages that were no longer active. In addition, the traffic did not show up in AdWords.

It was good that we identified the traffic in the first place. After some significant investigation, the traffic simply vanished. We never understood where it came from or why it left. We were also not charged for it. But had we not tracked it, it would have dramatically altered our weekly operating results, providing a false reading of performance for that week.

Low Traffic Volumes

A/B testing is often done to try to determine which of two slightly different website elements, such as a click-through ad, is more effective. In almost all online marketing operations, there are calls for A/B testing of nearly everything. In addition, since this is digital marketing, there is almost always the assumption that it is easy to pick out winners and losers in both conversions and referring site traffic. Unfortunately for most companies, there simply will not be enough site traffic to conduct meaningful A/B testing over a short-enough period of time. Even sites that generate 1,000+ visitors per day will find that A/B testing of pages takes an extremely long period of time to reach statistical relevance.

For companies that are in niche B2B segments, this lack of traffic also translates to keyword searches. Monthly global searches on niche keywords may be small enough that when click-through rates to the website are factored in, the amount of traffic arriving at the site barely registers on the site radar. Low traffic volumes simply complicate an already complex picture on most sites.

Correlation and Causation Bias

Without a deep understanding of what is happening on the company website, a CMO can get into trouble with sales leadership and the CEO. Even with sufficient traffic data to be statistically relevant, however, analyses of website traffic and the effect of marketing programs can be distorted when correlation and causation are confused.

Correlation occurs when two events happen and they appear to be linked. A major product launch occurs, for example, and during the product launch website traffic goes up 30%. On the surface, one could conclude that marketing did a tremendous job with the launch, causing more and more people to come to the website to check out what is new. However, correlation does not equal causation. Without deeper analysis of why site traffic increased, it is easy to assume this causation. In fact, however, the increase in site traffic could have been caused by something completely unrelated. Perhaps the email marketing team launched a major email blast on the day of the product launch. Perhaps the pay-per-click team increased the budget recently. Maybe an unrelated posting on a site drove referring site traffic that was completely unrelated to the product launch news.

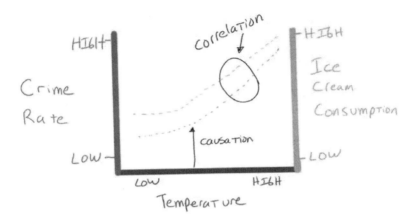

Figure 12: An increase in temperature has been shown to cause higher crime and higher ice cream consumption. But higher ice cream consumption doesn't cause more crime.

Falsely assuming causation for events which are only correlated can lead to all kinds of erroneous decisions and evaluations. However, there exists a causation bias to attribute changes in site traffic to recent events. Sometimes the answer to why something has changed is simply "we don't know." That is always a better answer than a causation assumption.

Size of the Data Sets and Application Performance

Ideally, all this data could be analyzed and linked and plotted in real time. The reality is much different. As we already mentioned, packages like Google Analytics will sample site traffic to reduce processing overhead. Marketing automation systems can churn and chug at queries at slow rates. While such a pace can be frustrating, they make sense when one considers the immense size of the datasets involved. These applications are working through enormous sets of clickstream and other data in a shared, multi-instance cloud application. The amount of money paid these vendors is rather modest when one considers the levels of computing power their customers can access. The downside remains, however. Performance for complex queries can be slow.

Over-Analysis and Tracking

It is possible to attempt to track so much data that it is actually very difficult to get a result. Theoretically, tracking every marketing tactic and every offer makes logical sense. On the surface, it would seem to make sense to determine exactly what white paper offer or webinar causes the most amount of closed deals. After all, CEOs want to know the secret sauce and the right offer to make. In B2B selling, though, rarely is there ever a clean path to a deal. Most deals involve multiple steps and offers. Most prospects respond to many different offers during the course of their engagement with the company. Tracking every action down to specific tactics and offers can create a situation in which it is impossible to identify broad categories of tactics that work. It is more valuable to understand that webinars that focus on particular topic areas appear to draw lots of interest and good opportunity creation rates than it is to understand exactly which webinar has the highest opportunity creation rate. Knowing which webinar is the best is not a problem, but it is important to understand exactly what you would do with any information gleaned from a metric before you decide to capture it. Capturing metrics has an overhead cost in terms of people, capture time, and also analysis time.

A company at which I worked tracked everything to great detail. The challenge lay in finding a trend of what was actually happening. Queries had to be expertly crafted to include the wide variety of programs in any analysis. Just this step alone complicated data analysis enough to make it far too difficult to get answers to basic queries.

Never track something unless you know what you will do with the results and what specific behavior may change based on those results. Otherwise, you risk complicating an already complex process without getting a tangible improvement in performance.

Lack of Analytics Capability

There is no substitute for understanding the details of traffic, conversions, and sales program follow-up. A bottom-up approach must occur in which the organization develops a deep understanding of what is happening across all stages of the lead pipeline process. This can only occur if all members of the marketing and sales teams are fully enabled and vested in the process. Enablement requires all members of the team to have access to key analytics packages, to know how to use the data coming from these packages, and to be able to synthesize the results into action for the rest of the team. Unfortunately, many marketing organizations either delegate analytics to a marketing team or a webmaster. The resulting lack of deep analytics knowledge prevents deep and insightful analysis of marketing operations.

Dashboarditis

The opposite of deep analytics capability is "dashboarditis". This disease occurs when executives and the marketing team believe that all metrics and numbers can be reduced to just a few short graphs or dashboards that will guide decision making. There certainly are key metrics that at an executive level can help guide an organization, but to get there these metrics must be built on an order of magnitude to ensure the organization is operating correctly and efficiently. Hitting weekly lead goals may not matter if the lead quality is low and the cost is high. Quick sales rep follow-up to new leads has no value if the sales team is just marking the leads as completed without making the required phone calls.

Dashboards can be extremely effective at measuring marketing and sales team effectiveness, but only if they are backed up by organizational depth in supporting metrics that can provide confidence that the dashboarded metric has value. Dashboards should be the final stop in the metrics process once all the hundreds of detailed measurement points have been completed and used to construct a solid foundation for the few key performance indicators (KPIs) that matter. Unfortunately, most organizations start by reviewing a few KPIs without developing the underlying foundation and falsely believe their results have value. Dashboards are good, but only once the metrics foundation has been built.

New Technologies, Communities

Even when the challenges noted above are overcome, B2B marketers still must face the constant pace of changing technologies, communities, and online marketing methods which add fresh complexity to marketing measurement. By the time you read this book, portions of it will be out of date and new sources of prospect generation will have become current.

The challenge is to stay on top of the trends, test them, and discard those processes that don't yield value. Of course given that technologies morph and change, even the ones that have been discarded require a return visit, especially if the community or technology continues to grow in scale. At one company at which I worked, we revisited Facebook advertising four different times over the course of two years. Such regular re-examinations were driven by changes to the Facebook advertising model and the continued growth of the platform.

Rising Above the Challenges

The many challenges faced by B2B marketers make it impossible for one report, or one dashboard, to reflect all aspects of marketing effectiveness. There is no one system, or process or community or marketing method, that works. B2B marketing is 60% science and metrics, and about 40% interpretation and educated guesses. Answers to inquiries from the CEO about whether a particular program is generating revenue can be difficult to provide. CEOs want simple answers. Very rarely does $100 put to work clearly translate to a particular amount of revenue in a clean, straightforward manner. By implying that this type of measurement is possible, a CMO can fall into a self-dug credibility hole. You can measure the impact of program spend to revenue, but the linkage is never as clean as some would like. Meanwhile, the art of reading results from a program is as important as the actual metrics.

The difficulties in tracing closed-loop marketing from program spend to revenue, however, don't provide an excuse to not take such measurements. On the contrary. Because there is no single, easy data point to use for tracking effectiveness, B2B marketers are forced to use multiple methods to measure effectiveness and apply the appropriate amount of interpretation. All members of the marketing team must be analytics enabled and must be willing to contribute their own analyses to the marketing process. Only then can a solid foundation of operational understanding be built. Only then can high-level dashboards and KPIs be constructed that allow senior-level decision makers to judge marketing effectiveness.

Which Atom Just Split to Make the Screw Turn?

Trying to determine which program or which traffic source or which website visitor contributed to a B2B sale is a little like the Captain walking into engineering and asking if we could determine which atom just split and ultimately caused the ship's screw to turn. We could certainly monitor how the reactor was operating and how the atoms were splitting. We could tell that all the control rods were working as they were supposed to. Based on this, we could see the reactor was generating heat that was then transferred to the primary coolant. We could monitor the steam generators and see they were transforming this primary coolant heat into steam. Then we could watch the steam flow through the pipes and hit the turbines. We could see the turbines spin and watch the ship's log go up as we moved through the water. So yes, the atoms splitting made the ship go. But which atom specifically caused a particular rotation of the screw would be pretty tough to determine.

Digital marketing is a bit like this. You can measure each segment of the process, but to try to tie the results of a sale all the way back to the one moment when an atom split — or a prospect clicked on an ad — would be difficult and not particularly useful. It is more important to measure each stage of the process with an understanding that, if you could get a prospect to the next stage, the programs applied to that stage would move that prospect forward in the process. It wasn't important to know which atom caused the screw to turn. But it was important to measure reactor output and how much steam was produced. If we could get the steam out of the reactor, we could convert it to the turbines spinning and making the boat go.

Take Action

- Look at some recently closed-deal forensics to try to reconstruct what actually happened from traffic source to closed deal. Pay attention to the programs, timing, and different actors required to get the deal closed.
- How does your company define a customer in the finance system? In the CRM system?
- What dashboards have been created for sales and marketing? Who uses them? What is valuable in these dashboards? Are they trusted?
- What is the newest marketing technique used by your team? How are results measured?

PART II: Traffic to Leads

The next three chapters get into details of how to measure site traffic and goal conversions on the website plus the nurturing process for leads. The chapters are detailed and get into nuances of measurement. If lead generation is not a concern, or you think your measurement of the traffic-to-lead part of the process is fine, then skip to Part III, Measuring Lead to Opportunity Conversion. Otherwise, read on!

Chapter 4: Measuring Site Traffic

What You Will Learn

In Chapter 2, we walked through a high-level overview of the different types of traffic that arrive on a marketer's website. In this chapter, we will develop a list of specific metrics for measurement. By the end of the chapter you will have a framework for evaluating all the different traffic sources. Traffic can be evaluated by how it came to the site, where it lands, and what it does while on the site. Each of these three measures is important to improving results from site traffic.

Overview – How, Where, What

All site traffic follows three general steps. Traffic is directed to the site, lands on the site, and travels around the site in some way.

Traffic can be directed to a website via:

- A link on another site
- An advertisement
- Results from a search engine query
- A link in someone's tweet
- A link on a community site
- The company name typed into a user's browser
- An email message with a link

Traffic to a site often contains information regarding its source such as the keyword used to conduct a search, the ad that resulted in a click-through, or even the name in the contact database to which an email was sent. This information can be used to subdivide overall site traffic into its various components (direct, inbound, etc.).

Once inbound traffic hits the site, it lands on a page called, simply enough, a landing page. The landing page could be custom-designed for the traffic, such as a page that is paired with an advertisement, or the landing page may be one with content of interest to which bloggers are linking. In many cases, the landing page may be the website's home page. Looking at landing pages, especially within the context of traffic sources, can help validate that traffic is classified correctly. It can also provide some insights into what pages people find interesting. This information can help site operators understand how the most qualified people may be arriving on the site.

Finally, once traffic arrives on the site, it may travel around a bit and accomplish a goal conversion. Since the purpose of traffic arriving on the site is to accomplish a goal, it is only logical to include goal conversion as part of any traffic measurement routine. The quality of the traffic that arrives on the site is directly related to the goal attainment percentage. Now goal attainment is also impacted by the layout of the site, the colors, content, the offers presented, and even site performance and other design factors. But holding the site structure and content constant over a given period, the goal conversion rate is a measure of the quality of traffic arriving at the site. If a site has three goals such as download white paper, download data sheet, and contact sales, for example, each traffic source should be measured across those goals.

As in other parts of digital marketing measurement, changes week over week in traffic and goal conversion rates may not be good or bad. Simply understanding why a change occurred can lead to valuable insights. A sudden increase in inbound traffic driven by investors reading an article in the local business section of a newspaper will increase traffic rates, but probably not goal conversion rates for "Contact Sales". In fact, for that week, the "Contact Sales" goal conversion rate will actually drop. The site isn't broken; the traffic quality has simply changed. In a later chapter we will look at measuring the impact of site design, structure, and content of the site as a whole on goal conversion rates.

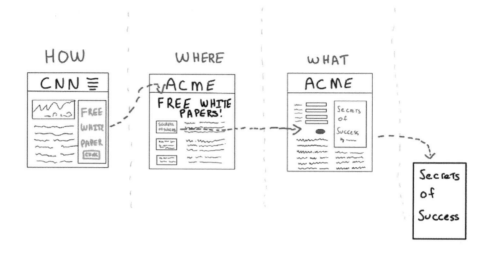

Figure 13: How: From an ad on CNN. Where: Home page. What: Over to a white paper offer page to download the white paper.

Segmentation = Accountability

The next step in measuring site traffic is to segment the traffic down to component parts. Segmentation of traffic is key to understanding site behavior, but it is also key to assigning accountability for traffic to marketing team members. Said another way, if the site needs to build traffic to increase leads to sales, it is difficult to build that traffic without specific individuals being accountable for driving traffic on a daily basis. In a later chapter, we will look at the marketing organization. However, as we introduce each metric here, we will also start to build up a list that details which team in the marketing organization is accountable for each metric. Without such accountability, no one may track a metric. Without anyone tracking a metric, there is no real way to drive behavior to change that metric's outcome.

Such a focus on attaching specific metrics to specific marketers may be refreshing, but it also represents a change in how many marketing teams operate. By attaching metrics and numbers to marketers, it becomes significantly easier to manage headcount. When the team is looked at in this manner, it becomes very painful for a CMO to add non-quota-carrying headcount to the team. What is better to do, for example, add a program manager to manage programs, or add another social media person who can drive additional traffic to the site and hence draw leads out of untapped communities?

Segmentation is critical for accurate measurement. It is also critical for accountability of metrics. With this in mind, let's dive into some traffic segmentation and measurements that the digital CMO may find of interest. Broadly speaking, we can segment traffic as either inbound or paid, and subdivide traffic flows even further within these categories.

Standing Watch as the Engineer

On the boat, our measurement of the boat's systems was divided up into specific areas for measurement and control. Without dividing what was a very complex operation problem into smaller sections with a person accountable for a specific area, it would be nearly impossible to operate the systems. The Engineering Officer, for example, divided the nuclear plant's operations into a few discrete measurement areas – reactor control, steam plant control, and electrical system control. The reactor made the steam, the steam plant converted it to turn the screw and made electricity, the electrical system distributed the power throughout the ship. Each process area was measured separately. Each area had its own crew member responsible for the operation. By dividing up the problem into smaller sections and assigning accountability for each area, control and measurement of a complex problem became measurable. The same holds for B2B marketing measurement.

Inbound Traffic

Inbound traffic is defined as traffic to a website that is not paid for. Its most basic form is direct traffic that comes directly to a website by someone typing in the URL of the website or clicking on a bookmarked link. Inbound traffic can also take the form of links to a website from other sites, making it referral traffic. Finally, search traffic originates when someone searches for a word or phrase and the site comes up in the organic search engine results page. Each of these traffic sources has its own unique measurements and quirks.

Direct Traffic

Direct traffic occurs when someone types in the URL of your site directly into a browser and lands on the site. The same sequence can also occur if they use a bookmark in their browser. Theoretically, direct traffic can represent a whole list of positive reasons for someone coming to a site.

Direct traffic should be a strong indicator of brand awareness and the stickiness of people wanting to return to your site. Unfortunately, without careful analysis of the site, this usually is not the case. Direct traffic may be reported by your analytics package as traffic with a source it can't determine. Although there are many ways for traffic to appear on a site without an apparent referring URL, many analytics packages take the easy way out and lump traffic without an apparent source into a general direct traffic category. This could result in a report of a significant amount of direct traffic when in fact most of that traffic is not direct at all. Traffic originating from email marketing programs that arrives without the email marketing codes, for example, may appear as direct traffic on a site when it is not.

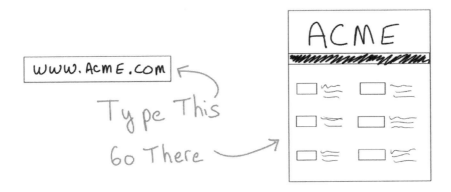

Figure 14: Direct traffic is fairly simple. Type in an address into the browser and you show up at a site. But what direct traffic really means is that it can't be resolved to a specific source.

Search engines also steal what would normally be direct traffic. End user behavior is such that many prospects will simply type the company name, not the company's URL, into the search box or address box on the browser. If a name is typed into the search box, a search engine will resolve it into the URL and the direct traffic will become SEO (search engine optimization) traffic. Or, if the company is running branded pay-per-click ads, the prospect may click a PPC ad on the search results page and show up as paid traffic. If the prospect types the company name into the address bar rather than the search box, depending on the browser this action may call up a search engine results page and the traffic will get categorized as search engine-related.

Direct traffic, in other words, is a catch-all for traffic that can't be resolved in any other way. Despite this, direct traffic is a useful metric. They key is to first strip out non-direct traffic from the measure and create an adjusted direct traffic metric. Creating this metric requires some advanced work in Google Analytics or another analytics package. To do this, look at all direct traffic, but through the lens of the landing pages the traffic is hitting. If traffic is arriving at landing pages with URLs designed to be landing pages for paid advertising, you can probably guess this is not direct traffic. If traffic is landing on obscure URLs deep in your site, most likely this is not direct traffic. The key is to logically check to see if the page upon which people are landing might have been typed into a browser as a direct URL. For this reason, there are two key measures that must be taken into consideration in addition to goal conversion rate. The first is the amount of direct traffic. The second measure involves looking at the top landing pages for direct traffic on a monthly basis, then comparing month-over-month and 90-day plus over-90-day traffic trends for these pages. The final step, of course, requires measuring the goal conversion rate for this direct traffic.

A spreadsheet containing all the metrics referenced in this book can be downloaded from www.storymetrix.com/resources. This sheet will be referenced often in this book.

Referring Site Traffic

Referring site traffic is just what the name implies. Another website has decided to link to your website. By doing so, it not only will send traffic to your site, but will also communicate to Google that your site is special for some reason. Legitimate referring site links can be created for a multitude of reasons, and link building itself is an entire domain of expertise. Some reasons for links include:

- **Press Releases** – Every digital press release issued today features the ability to include links back to the issuing company.

- **Bloggers Like Your Content** – A great blog posting or interesting product information that catches a blogger's eye may result in them writing a post and including links to your site.
- **Press Articles and Analysts** – Traditional press stories published online may include links to companies or specific products mentioned in an article. In addition to reporters with specific product and service beats, analysts write about industry developments of interest to their readers.
- **Community Postings and Comments** – Many community-oriented sites are vibrant enough that end users post problems in the hope that someone will assist them with an answer. If your website contains the answer, a community member may post a link to your site.
- **Tweets** – For many users, Twitter is their conversational platform during the course of the day. When they come across an interesting article online or a piece of content they like, they may post a tweet and include a link. Other Twitter users who follow the original poster or follow the topic area may see the tweet and click on the link to arrive on your website. If they like what they see, they may retweet the original tweet or write their own.

There are many other ways to build links, some not so effective and others just plain slippery and brand eroding. Most effective are the links created by end users not associated with your company who like something on your site. The role of content is critical for link building and inbound traffic.

While measuring referring site traffic in aggregate is important, real insights come from peeling back the referring site traffic and understanding its component parts. Generally, referring site traffic can be grouped as coming from:

- **Press, Analysts, and Bloggers** – These range from niche press sites to more mainstream sites like NYTimes.com and include analysts and bloggers who write content related to your industry
- **Community Sites** – Twitter, LinkedIn, Facebook, YouTube and niche communities
- **Other** – All other sources of traffic out there

Of course for a particular industry there may be different groupings of referring site traffic. The key is to further subdivide the section into component parts both for tracking and accountability.

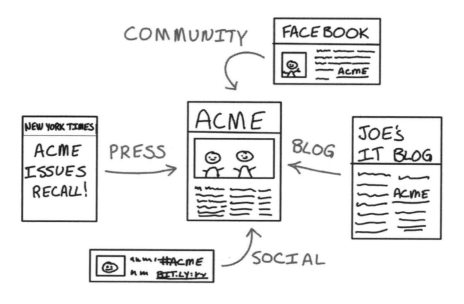

Figure 15: Blogs, community postings, traditional press links, links from tweets all drive referring site traffic.

Press, Analysts, and Bloggers

Analyst, press, and bloggers (APB) are to some extent grouped together when it comes to online analysis. Theoretically, all three of these groups consist of online writers who publish material on various topics and are generally categorized as influencers. The lines between them can be somewhat blurry. In some markets, well-placed industry analyst commentary drives significant credibility and traffic. In other markets, buyers tend to trust their favorite online bloggers when it comes to product reviews. In many cases, traffic driven by bloggers can dwarf traffic driven by traditional media. The beauty of digital marketing lies in its ability to reveal who has the strength and influence and who just appears to have the reach.

Core measurements for these traffic sources track the amount of traffic they create and their respective conversion rates. Segmenting these sources down to A-, B-, and C-level influencers also helps determine whether you are maximizing mind share with the key target influencers. A-level influencers would theoretically have the greatest ability to drive traffic to your site. The same goes for those classified as B- and C-level influencers. With enough focus and work, a marketing team can establish a validated list of the real A-, B-, and C-level influencers based on ability to drive traffic. This provides an invaluable focus point for relationship building with influencers who matter.

Of course, with press and analyst relations, there may be strategic and awareness goals associated with a particular person. So while a certain person may not drive traffic, there may be very valid reasons to pursue a relationship and get articles and commentary published by that person. The key is to understand which relationships fall into this strategic or awareness category and which relationships help drive traffic. Understanding this categorization also helps to assign budget resources. Each strategic analyst or press person requires some amount of time to manage and feed the relationship. A trade-off will occur between spending money that is strategic versus spending money that drives traffic and leads.

Once the list of key influencers is built, constantly revalidating the categorization of each influencer is important. Comparing month-over-month and quarter-over-quarter traffic by site helps to validate continued effectiveness of the sites at driving traffic. Since these sites are dependent on their own traffic to even be able to refer traffic to another site, if an A blogger site starts losing readership, it won't matter how many great articles they write with links to your site, the traffic they refer to your site will go down. Hence, in addition to tracking absolute traffic from these sites, comparing trailing 90-day-over-90-day traffic, and 180-day-over-180-day traffic by referring website is critical to your ability to pick up on reductions in traffic. If a reduction is detected, then it is important to determine if the cause is from:

- Loss of influencer mindshare due to a lack of outreach
- A blogger who just doesn't find your stuff interesting
- A reduction in the blogger's own traffic

In addition to looking at the sites that are sending traffic your way, examining the actual URLs or stories that contain links to your site is also extremely valuable. Abnormally high traffic from a blog may indicate great interest in a particular topic from that blogger's readership. Indicators of hot topics represent invaluable market intelligence that can be used in product decisions, content creation decisions, and other marketing programs.

The Dutch Disappear

At a startup company where I worked, we had the good fortune of dramatically increasing our referring site traffic month over month and year over year. But all was not well, and we didn't realize it until we started to look at the quarter-over-quarter numbers for referring sites. What we saw was that a giant long tail of referring sites was driving up our traffic numbers. But a key Dutch blogger site, equal to about half the long tail traffic, had basically stopped writing about us. Although our referring site traffic metric was going way up, if we had kept this blogger engaged with us our traffic would have been even higher due to his stature. There is never enough traffic, so although we were growing, we set about figuring out what had happened.

After unsuccessful attempts by various people to reach out to the blogger, we realized our coverage drop somewhat coincided with the departure of our company's founder. The more we investigated, the more clear it became that the founder had been the primary contact and spokesperson for this blogger.

The blogger didn't like being handed off to a non-founder. Hence, we had broken the relationship. From this we learned to subdivide traffic in some cases down to individual sites and to make sure everyone understands who is responsible for maintaining key relationships with site operators. This step can be critical to maintaining and continuing to grow traffic.

Community Sites

Loosely defined, online communities are sites where end users congregate to swap information, seek advice, or share content. Facebook is a community. YouTube is a community video sharing site. VMware Community is a vibrant community of virtual machine technologists. Reddit is a social news website that is more community than news site. Companies can also develop their own communities that are either branded with the company name or a separate entity. Regardless of how communities are constructed, they drive traffic to themselves. Some of this traffic can end up on your corporate website if your site contains content the community finds relevant or interesting.

When a community represents a gathering place for potential prospects, its site can be an invaluable source of traffic and sales leads. However, vendors are usually not welcome to post or participate. Luckily this is not always the case. In some instances vendors can participate, provided they are adding value to the community and not promoting products. If a company produces value-added content for an industry, community members may reference a vendor's content and link to a vendor site to answer specific questions posed by community members. Likewise, a vendor can also answer questions many times by pointing to information provided on its own site. Of course, for a company lucky enough to have built a community of enthusiasts that also aligns with their products, that community can provide significant free traffic that can then be exposed to the vendor's products in subtle ways.

Similar to the way referring site URLs can provide market information about hot topics, community posts that provide the most traffic to a company's site can reveal which problems or questions arise among their prospects most often.

This information can then serve as a basis for product ideas or future white papers and blog posts.

Many communities award points to posters who answer questions most effectively or who post frequent content that is appreciated by other community members. Product evangelists who are tasked to participate in prospect communities can be measured on their contributions to a community with such a point system.

Community Long Tail

A company where I worked used community outreach for both lead generation and to be involved in the community and more aware of the market. Analyzing our community traffic over time, we discovered that no single posting was driving significant traffic over a given week or even month. But over many months and many postings, the total traffic from all the communities continued to climb. The growth came from a hundred or so different postings, with each posting contributing a small number of visitors. This long tail of traffic was very hard to build, but it turned out to be very sustainable over time. It also continued to reinforce that there is rarely one magic post or contribution or blog comment that suddenly unleashes traffic onto a site. Slow and steady always seems to be the process required to gradually build a following and traffic.

Search Engines

Search engines, primarily Google, are another source of traffic for B2B websites. Users who type search queries into Google receive listings of results. Paid results are the ads that may appear in the first few positions of the page and on the right side of the page. When a search is performed, Google returns rank-order results based on the relevance of the search term and the relevance of the sites returned. The higher a site's ranking in the results, the more traffic the site will get from users searching on the query. The drop-off of meaningful traffic from the first position to the tenth position is dramatic. Traffic generated from results on the second page of organic search results is even lighter. For such reasons, gaining a spot on the top of search results, based on Google deciding that your site is the most relevant for a particular search term, can drive significant amounts of generally highly qualified, free traffic.

Figure 16: Searchers typing "Product Recall" into Google will get results based on a site's domain strength and how relevant the content on that site is to the query.

Of course your site has to rank high for a term and there has to be a significant number of monthly global searches for the term. Like other aspects of online marketing mentioned in this book, search engine marketing is its own specialty. The goal here is to equip the CMO or marketing VP with a basic understanding of what to measure and what it means so the maximum volume of qualified traffic can be driven.

There are two ways to impact search engine rankings. The first is called onsite optimization. The second method is through offsite methods that prompt other websites to point to your site as the source of information for particular topics. For onsite optimization, search engines send crawlers to websites to index the sites and build their search databases. Onsite strategies ensure the crawlers properly index the site and capture the relative importance of a page and its content relative to other pages on the site. Top-level pages, header tags, and URLs that match specific keywords represent just some of the ways site structure communicates to search engines regarding what content on a site is important. Onsite SEO is an art unto itself with its own universe of consultants, books, and blogs dedicated to optimization.

While search engines rely on a site's structure to determine what a site owner believes is important on a site, search engines also rely on the links and pointers contained in other sites to determine how important others in the world think a website may be for a particular topic. This is the realm of offsite SEO. The more valuable content published by a website that is referenced by other sites, the more the site's domain authority in the world is boosted for a particular topic area. The more Facebook "Likes" and Google +1 ratings are given to a site, the higher the amount of social acceptance drives relevance as far a search engine is concerned. These are just some of the basic measures in an ever-evolving technology.

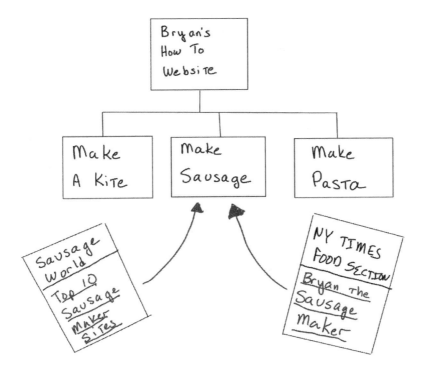

Figure 17: Bryan's How To site has "How to Make Sausage" as a top-level page. This tells Google that Bryan thinks this content is valuable. More importantly, both Joe's Blog and the NYTimes.com have linked to this page.

To support offsite search engine optimization and other projects, a sound content publishing strategy is critical. Content publishing strategies typically involve a frequent cadence of blog posts, rich website content including videos, a strong social presence, publication of white papers, speaking engagements, online community participation, and a strong press and industry analyst outreach program. The weight, balance, and success of each of these programs will vary by industry. Essentially, however, the more others are talking about you and point at your site as a trusted source of information on a topic, the higher your site's ranking in search engine results.

Measuring success with SEO at a high level involves simply measuring the amount of traffic generated from search engines. Theoretically, as content is produced and a website's stature in the industry increases due to its thought leadership, the amount of free search engine traffic for relevant topics should increase.

There are generally three types of traffic provided by Google. Branded SEO traffic is traffic that contains your brands' or products' names in the search terms. Given that your website is where these products or brands are offered, supported, and talked about in great detail, there should be no surprise that if a user searches on one of your brands, Google will list this as a top search result and people will click this link since they identify your site and your brand as excellent resources. Individual branded search words should include all product names, company names, and other terms that are unique to a company. Separating these words out from the other search terms when reporting SEO results helps provide a true picture of how well an SEO program is operating. Theoretically, if a company is growing its awareness, branded SEO will just grow.

Non-branded SEO traffic is the opposite of branded. Non-branded search terms are most likely from the domain area of your products and services. It is more challenging to get traffic from these terms since your competitors are also talking about and publishing content with the hope of attracting SEO traffic for these terms. For digital cameras, terms such as digital camera, f-stop, and shutter speed are used everywhere by everyone. Any number of camera manufacturers compete to drive traffic to their sites using these and other camera-related non-branded search terms.

Tracking and understanding traffic generated by non-branded keywords, however, does provide invaluable insights into what your potential customers are searching for online. Looking at long tail search results can be especially enlightening. Long tail search terms contain multiple words strung together. So while there may be massive competition for search engine ranking on "Best SUV" among car manufacturers, "Best SUV with towing capacity of 6,000 lbs" may have much lower competition and daily searches, but result in more highly qualified traffic. If you happen to be a car manufacturer with an SUV with 6,000 lbs of towing capacity and you notice traffic coming in from this search, it may be time to call in your SEO expert and figure out how to boost your rankings through both onsite and offsite techniques in order to drive even more traffic to your site.

The third category of Google search engine traffic comes from keywords that are "not provided". When a prospect signs into Google and does a search, Google no longer provides the keywords used in the search to the referenced site. While this is still a relatively new phenomenon, "not provided" it is starting to represent a growing portion of SEO traffic.

Going Deeper with Keywords

Tracking the overall trending of search traffic over time is important to understanding how well as a whole your website is doing at generating organic search traffic. Analysis of the underlying keywords driving such traffic deserves its own section. Keywords are both the short and long terms that people type into search engines. How well a company's site ranks on a particular keyword as the source of information to resolve that search represents the company's keyword ranking. If you type iPhone into Google, the top search result will be from Apple. Why? Apple has a top-10 domain rank as a site of value on the web. Apple.com has pages called /iPhone, and there are literally millions of sites that most likely point to Apple with links referring to the iPhone. In Google's eyes, someone searching for iPhone should probably be directed to Apple.com first to find an answer to their query.

Creating a list of queries or keywords that will most likely attract qualified prospects is the first step in developing a keyword list for your company. Keyword development is an art in and of itself, with many books written about how to develop an effective list. Whatever process is adopted to tackle this task, the goal should be to develop a list of keywords that will be used to drive qualified search traffic to the site. Once this keyword list is developed, most SEO applications provide the ability to track keyword rankings over time.

If most of a site's traffic arrives through long tail keyword searches, short keyword rankings may not be relevant. In addition, monthly traffic projections provided by third-party tools for keywords may not be accurate. Say your number-one target keyword has 10,000 monthly searches, and you are sitting in the first position for results. Expecting 10% of the 10,000 searches might seem logical, leading to an expectation of 1,000 visitors as SEO traffic from this specific keyword each month. However, many variables could make this math inaccurate.

The first variable involves the actual monthly traffic estimate. Running a paid campaign on a keyword is one of the more accurate ways to determine true traffic volume. The second variable is the web page summary presented beneath the keyword in the search results. While your website listing may appear near the top of the results page, most prospects will still read the information presented by the search engine prior to deciding whether to click on your listing. If you are attempting to drive site traffic based on a keyword that is heavily branded by a competitor, or a derivation of that keyword, prospects searching for that term may simply trust and be more attracted to the brand's owner rather than your site listing. All of these factors influence the amount of traffic specific keywords actually drive to your site.

Keyword Rankings Might Not Matter

A competitor of ours was ranked number one for a keyword deemed especially important by our CEO and board. Each week, animated discussions took place around why we did not rank as well as this company for this particular keyword. Ultimately, the competitor purchased us. As soon as I had access to their keywords, I investigated the amount of traffic they received from this valuable keyword they were dominating. Answer? Less than 10 visitors per week on a projected volume of about 1,000. The lesson learned here: Projections for traffic based on keyword ranking can vary wildly. What we perceived to be so important and such an important driver for traffic was actually having little to no impact on the competitive landscape.

Tracking Content Production

Measuring inbound traffic is critical. Measuring the input to the inbound traffic equation is just as important. Content is generally what drives links, referring site traffic, Twitter mentions, press releases, analyst mentions, etc. Measuring content production is therefore critical in any top-level measurement of marketing effectiveness.

Good content starts as a concept or content idea. It could be an idea for a white paper, video, or blog series. This starting kernel of an idea is then reproduced and distributed across multiple channels. It is this multi-channel distribution that impacts the site traffic measurements mentioned above.

For example, let's assume it's January 2013 and someone in the marketing department of a company that makes power control equipment has the idea that a discussion of the power outage at the 2013 Super Bowl would be timely. Since the company makes power control equipment, a content idea surfaces around "15 Common Mistakes Configuring Power Control Equipment that can Cause an Outage". A content producer creates the content initially in the form of a white paper. The white paper is then sliced up into blog postings. Each of these postings is then distributed through Twitter and RSS feeds and promoted in emails. A video interview is produced with the author of the white paper. A press release is issued that also results in a press interview. Community sites in which the power outage is discussed by power experts are monitored and, where appropriate, product evangelists contribute commentary and potentially link to any valuable content that builds the conversation. Finally, a quick podcast update is created. From the single topic of a power outage, multiple pieces of content are created that provide a series of opportunities for link creation back to the company site.

There are two ways to track such content production. One is to count the individual mentions, tweets, articles, blog postings, etc. each week. The greater the quantity of these items each week, the better. The second way is to develop a weighted content production number. For each piece of content produced, a weighting is assigned to the content. An outbound tweet, for example, may be one point whereas a complete white paper is 10. By weighting each of the pieces of content, a weighted total of content produced can be calculated each week as a measure of exactly how much the team is producing.

Paid Advertising

While organic traffic is always desirable, it may not be possible to grow the business on organic traffic alone. Especially when a little-known company is attempting to gain awareness in a market dominated by larger players, attempting to produce more content than the larger players in order to gain high search engine rankings may not be successful. Paid advertising, however, does enable a company of any size to reach new audiences.

There are multiple ways to invest money to drive leads for sales. Paid search places ads on search results pages and on contextually relevant pages throughout the web on a pay-for-performance basis. Traditional online banner advertising provides impressions with no guarantee of click-through rate. These cost-per-impression (PPM) campaigns could be delivered online or through email sponsorships or even outright email blasts sent through third parties.

In addition to methods to drive traffic to a website for conversion, various pay-per-lead (PPL) schemes exist through which media companies provide names of people who have downloaded white papers or in other ways expressed interest in a company's products. These media companies drive these leads through their own use of banner advertising, content, and emails on their own sites. Outright list purchases of names for cold calling or emails is another method to drive leads and website traffic. Finally, trade shows and other physical events represent a 100% offline method of lead generation. All of these paid methods will ultimately result in some level of traffic going to a website as prospects seek to learn more about the company. Each method of paid traffic then needs to be analyzed for success so the proper allocation of resources can be made.

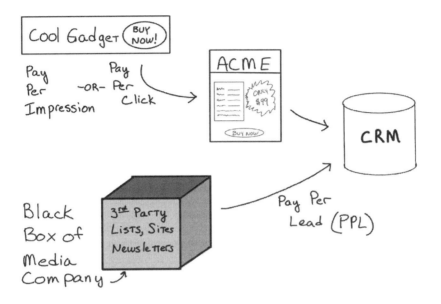

Figure 18: PPM charges based on impressions only with no guarantee of clicks. PPC only charges based on clicks. PPL is a turn-key program that delivers leads directly to a company's CRM system.

Pay-Per-Click Advertising

Entire books have been written on PPC advertising that cover how to do it and how to measure it. The goal here is to provide the CMO with a basic outline of how to understand and interpret results of PPC advertising.

PPC has the potential to be the highest daily spend for a marketing organization. In addition, PPC spending can be highly dynamic. As such, it requires significant scrutiny on a weekly basis by management if PPC spend represents a large amount of budget or a high percentage of the total budget. PPC spending has the potential to provide invaluable market intelligence if analyzed correctly.

First, some definitions. PPC advertising for this book will refer to Google AdWords since it completely dominates online ad spending. Within pay-per-click advertising there are several areas of spending – search, content network, and remarketing.

Search Advertising

Search-based advertising places ads on search result pages based on the relevance of the search term typed into the search box. Ad position on the page is one factor in click-through rates to your site, as is the amount of the bid relative to other advertisers and the success of the ad at generating interest. In addition, search engine sites like Google display ads that generate clicks and revenue for them. So even having the highest bid ad does not guarantee success. Said another way, since Google is a pay-for-performance ad system, you can be the highest bidder for a search term which theoretically should guarantee you placement near the top of the page, but if no one ever clicks on your ad, Google will not display your ad since they make no money on it. If this is the case, you may be forced to give up your ad's highly desirable position.

Google search advertising is highly controlled, easy to track, and fairly straightforward. By purchasing search terms, marketers can research search volumes, test what people click on, and test product messaging through ad copy.

Google provides massive amounts of data that can be used to evaluate, tune, and change advertising. As a CMO, how do you determine what segments of such data are important to monitor? The following should be at the top of your list and are discussed below:

- Spending on a weekly basis
- Changes in click-through rates
- Goal conversions rate

- Lost impression share due to budget
- Lost impression share due to ad quality
- Unique campaign spending
- Overall ranking of campaign success

Spending on a weekly basis represents an important number to watch as a measure of budget outflow. It is also important to see whether this spending results in the sales opportunities it's designed to produce. If you suddenly start spending a lot of money and the opportunity creation does go up, be concerned.

The second important area of measurement involves changes in click-through rates. Click-through rate (CTR) is the percentage of people who see an ad and click. The higher the overall CTR, the more successful the marketing team has been in placing the right ad with the right message in front of the right prospects.

The next measurement area involves the need to understand the conversion rate on the website and to calculate a cost/goal. Since PPC advertising can be used to drive all types of goals, it is important to measure separately the cost/goal for each of these areas. If it costs $300 to get someone to the website ready to read some content and click "Contact Sales", but only $10 to get someone to the website to download a white paper, this is important data to know. The next step would be to determine how many people who read the white paper go on to click "Contact Sales". If 10% of the white paper downloads click "Contact Sales", then spending $300 to get 30 people to download a white paper, of which 10% (three people) will eventually click "Contact Sales" makes more sense than spending $300 to get one sales prospect by appealing directly for the "Contact Sales" close. Clearly driving people to white papers, in this example, would be the way to go at a cost of $100/lead.

Goal conversion measurement has its own nuances. A vast majority of traffic responding to an ad will land on a page and bounce off. A smaller amount of traffic will either complete the action called for on the page, or escape the page to other sections of the website where they could complete different actions.

Understanding how goal conversions are measured is important to consistently measuring advertising effectiveness. One method is to only measure conversions that take place on the landing page. Other methods of tracking look for conversions that occur anywhere on the website, provided the original traffic arrived from an ad. Either way is acceptable as long as the method is consistent across all numbers reported.

Beyond cost-per-goal-conversion tracking, there are some administrative areas in search marketing that also make sense to track. First is lost impression share due to budget. Within PPC advertising, budgets are set for spending. When you hit your weekly budget, Google slows down the serving of your ads. The result is lost impression share as a result of budget. If you had more money, Google would spend it for you. If you are having success with conversion rates, it helps to know that you are missing impressions due to budget on a weekly basis when allocating resources.

In addition to lost share due to budget, you can also lose share due to ad quality. In this type of scenario you have sufficient budget for ads, but no one is clicking on them. Hence Google decides to not place your ad on a page if another ad that makes them more money is available. This is known as lost impression share due to ad quality. This is a good measure of the ability of your PPC team to create compelling ads with high click-through rates based on the right keywords.

The tracking mentioned so far has been at the aggregate level of PPC spending. Search engine marketers, however, actually divide their program spend into unique campaigns that have unique keywords and advertising associated with them. Getting into the details of how each campaign is performing is probably too weedy for marketing leadership to dive into. However, understanding which campaigns consume the most budget dollars, deliver the most impressions, and have the highest click-through rates and highest goal conversion rates is critical from a market intelligence standpoint.

Let's get back to the tractor company example we used earlier in the book. If your company is selling 4-ton front loaders, it would seem logical to place an ad using the keyword "4-Ton Front Loader". By looking at impressions and impression share, you can validate how many times people are actually searching on "4-Ton Front Loader". You might find, for example, that people, for whatever reason, tend to search ten times as often for "5-Ton Front Loader" than they do for a 4-ton loader. What does this tell you? It is not clear except to say that a 4-ton loader is not as top of mind as a 5-ton loader. Perhaps people aren't aware a smaller tractor exists, or perhaps the market leader in the space only sells 5-ton loaders. Either way, such information can inform future marketing decisions. Maybe it is time to make a 4-ton front loader or convince the market that a 5-ton loader is just too big.

Overall ranking of campaign success is also important to understand. Suppose you created a series of solution campaigns. One campaign was around "loading gravel into a truck", the other campaign was "digging a hole", while the final campaign was "snow removal". In each of these campaigns, ads were run that appealed to people looking for a tractor to solve the problem presented. Searching for "tractor to dig hole" might serve up an ad that says "Best Tractor for Digging Holes" with a link to the site and a white paper talking about the hole-digging capacity of the 4-ton tractor. By looking at the traffic and impressions delivered by these ads, you can derive some measure of how often people are searching for these solutions online, and potentially devise a rank order for which problems customers use the tractors to solve. Caution must be used to not jump to conclusions on the data, but such data should be considered too interesting to ignore and not probe.

Ad Network

While search advertising is a very controlled environment in which ads based on keyword criteria entered into the Google search bar are displayed, Google also operates an ad network that is a bit different. The Google Display Network, and many competing ad networks, operate by paying website operators to display ads. Network operators give the website operators a cut of the revenue generated by these ads. Ads are selected for display on a website based on content on the site. Such ad network attempt to match ads with website content. On a given day, much more ad space is available on these ad networks than on search results pages. Ads placed on these networks can go to tens of thousands of sites, creating the potential for massive website traffic. PPC experts know how to get results from this type of content network. But, as a CMO, how do you determine what should be tracked? Top of the list: ad network traffic and ad network bounce rates.

While ad networks can provide significant traffic to a website, such traffic tends to be very unqualified. Understanding how much of a website's total traffic is driven by ad networks in a given week is critical to understanding overall traffic numbers.

Since ad network traffic tends to be lower quality than other sources, monitoring the bounce rate for the landing pages of this traffic can provide an early indication of quality. A user "bounces" when they hit a page, then immediately exit. Tracking bounce rates for ad network traffic is important as fraud, bad placements, or ads that drive the wrong type of traffic can expend significant budget quickly. Since bounce rates track people who hit the site and immediately leave, understanding weekly goal conversion rates is also important.

Finally, looking at the top referring domains provides perhaps the most meaningful measure of the quality of traffic created via an ad network. While this segment of traffic may be too detailed for a CMO report, the PPC team should know exactly which domains are driving ad network traffic. Domains that make no sense for PPC should be blocked before significant budget is expended.

Shady Domains

While running an ad network campaign, we found significant traffic coming from domains that theoretically should have our prospects on them. Since we sold software to IT administrators, online gaming sites, shareware sites, and general-purpose IT sites seemed to be good domains for our ad networks to leverage. Over time, however, the goal conversion rates were exceptionally low, as were the opportunities generated from these conversions. While we were getting some conversions and mega traffic, it soon became clear that the network sites were not attracting our prospects. At this point we reconfigured much of the ad network program, which resulted in a massive drop in top-line site traffic. This quickly led to conversations at management meetings as to why "site traffic dropped". For traffic-obsessed CEOs and boards, changes in traffic can be alarming. But testing network sites and eventually shutting off those that weren't resulting in sales opportunities was the right decision. In hindsight, not telegraphing the experiment and the fact that traffic volumes could drop represented a missed opportunity to both educate the management team and keep expectations set correctly.

Remarketing

Remarketing is one of the more interesting areas in digital advertising. As in many parts of this book, the content here could become out-of-date shortly, but the measurement techniques will not. Remarketing refers to the ability to record someone's preference for a particular website or product area and serve up ads based on this preference when the prospect leaves the site in an attempt to get them back and engaged in the sales process.

In the business-to-consumer world, remarketing is easy to explain. If you visit an ecommerce site, look at an electric razor, and then depart the site, the ecommerce site knows that you are looking at electric razors. When you depart the site and land on another website that allows for network advertising, the original ecommerce site can request that these networks track you and display ads for the electric razor you saw on its site. Remarketing is in its infancy and will develop as advertisers learn what actually makes people return to and re-engage with a website. Remarketing metrics should be reported differently than other types of online pay-for-performance advertising since remarketing really targets a different type of prospect. An advertiser could vary the type of offer presented via remarketing as well as the frequency of ads. When these two items are fine tuned, the standard metrics of traffic and click-through rates can be applied. Remarketing has the ability to be extremely effective for B2B marketers.

Pay-Per-Image Advertising

Unlike pay-per-click advertising, PPM represents impression-based, old-school advertising. Prior to Google-based search advertising, most internet advertising was impression based. For a certain amount of money, advertisers would receive so many displays or impressions of their ads. Clicks were the responsibility of the advertiser, as were conversions. PPM advertising puts nearly the entire burden for ad performance on the advertiser.

Other forms of advertising, while not explicitly PPM, are essentially PPM based. Advertising in emails or even renting third-party email lists and sending out blind emails is essentially still PPM based. In each of these examples, some sort of impression for your product is delivered to a set number of addresses.

In all PPM cases, the first key metric is to understand the click-through rate on the traffic generated to the website, and the conversion rate once traffic hits the website. While cost/impression is interesting from an awareness standpoint, it is difficult to argue that generating awareness without a click has value. Theoretically, a well-constructed ad can generate awareness at a minimum and clicks in the very best case. Cost/impression is useful for budgeting and to determine the required click-through rate an ad would have to produce to make the campaign hit the required ROI.

While an ad's click-through rate is important to measure, a click's value only becomes monetized if the prospect takes action and converts on the target website. For this reason, cost per goal conversion is really the critical measure. Advertising campaigns operated on a PPM basis on non-relevant websites can generate clicks that do not convert or, worse, no clicks at all.

Website sponsorships represent another form of PPM advertising. In this case, a site may offer sponsorship of specific real estate on another website for a specific fee that is billed on a monthly or quarterly basis. This is essentially another form of PPM without the impression count. Understanding approximate website traffic to the sites being sponsored allows conversion of the sponsorship cost to a cost/impression for comparison purposes. However, many small sites may have unaudited traffic statistics, making a reliable traffic number difficult to acquire. In some cases, website sponsorships may be undertaken to get access to a blogger or site operator for strategic and other purposes.

Third-Party Spamming

Classic banner advertising had not worked for us in several years. Blog sponsorships, however, worked well, though not from a click-through or even conversion perspective. Instead, they worked due to their ability to generate some measure of coverage on sponsored blogs. The monthly check to the blog site operator at least kept the company name and product top of mind.

Using third-party lists for email marketing was another story. We found several legitimate, third-party emailing outfits that would take our content and mail it out on our behalf to their database based on the selects we provided. The results were strong, the click-through rates made sense, and the conversion rates were acceptable. However, we started to notice over time that our prospects had the perception that we were spamming people. Plus unsubscribes from our own database were starting to go up. It turned out that the third-party vendor database had significant overlap with our extensive homegrown list. By using a third-party list, we were double-mailing our own database in some cases. We discontinued the practice despite the short-term drop-off in leads and the resulting friction with the sales team over their drop in lead volume.

Pay-Per-Lead

PPL or pay-per-lead programs represent another entire industry in and of itself. In PPL, third-party content sites use their own internal email lists and website traffic to directly generate leads for the advertiser. White papers, software downloads, samples, calculators – all kinds of offers are used to get people to express interest and take an action. The resulting names are then sent to the advertiser for follow-up.

In some cases, the content site can actually send the traffic back to the advertiser's site for form conversion and fulfillment, with the advertiser paying on a cost-per-conversion basis. But this set-up is abnormal. In PPL programs, generally an up-front commitment is made both in terms of money to the content site and leads from the content site to the advertiser.

Key metrics to understand are the cost/name or lead, data quality, and opportunity conversion rates. We will discuss opportunity conversion rates in later chapters, but nowhere is it more important to measure data quality and opportunity conversion rates than with PPL programs. The challenge with offsite third-party programs involves the fact that your interests and the advertiser's interests are not necessarily 100% aligned. Your company is looking for sales-ready leads, or at least potential prospects who can be nurtured into sales-ready leads. The advertiser, on the other hand, is working to utilize as little of its advertising inventory as possible to get plausible names to the company. The challenge here is that normal lead-to-opportunity conversion rates are generally well below 20%. With a small sample size of leads from the vendor, a couple of "good leads" that the sales team is excited about can overshadow an expensive, costly, and inefficient program.

A secondary challenge involves the nature of the action taken by the potential prospect. Whatever action a prospect takes usually happens on the third-party site, where the company has little control over branding. A sales rep contacting a prospect may draw no connection between the sales rep's company name and the action taken to become a prospect.

Direct Mail

No discussion of paid programs and traffic would be complete without a quick discussion of direct mail. Even in an online B2B marketing operation, direct mail has its place and many marketers continue to use it. Direct mail linked to website offers can provide an easy way to bridge the offline/online gap. Assuming the call to action is online oriented, tracking cost/conversion and comparing these costs to other channels can provide ready insights into whether direct mail can work for a target market.

A software company where I worked was selling into a highly technical, 100% online, highly social media-driven audience. It was not uncommon to go to a conference and have all the audience members talking amongst themselves on Twitter during a presentation. Members of this target audience did not get much snail mail at work, a fact that translated into an opportunity. A cheap postcard promoting the company's best offer had a 2% click-through rate from the postcard to the website, and a nearly 30% conversion rate from the site to the action. Overall, the cost to deliver the required action was less than online AdWords spending, an impressive result from a direct mail campaign to a very technical audience.

Events

Events can be classified as either offline or online. Measurement of offline events is important since ultimately these prospects end up online due to event follow-up campaigns. Online events tend to be webinars which take the trade show presentation format and move it online. Beyond webinars, multi-day online seminars are also possible, along with completely online trade shows.

Online

Measurement and tracking for online events divides into two categories depending on the party responsible for driving traffic and registrations for the event. If a third party is used to drive registrations, this type of online event looks similar to a pay-per-lead program. Rather than drive white paper registrations, in this case, the third party is guaranteeing registrations and attendance at a webinar. If the company is 100% responsible for their own webinar, then the event starts to look like any other goal conversion event. Understanding the dynamics of the event is important in determining what to measure.

For third-party events, the same metrics used for PPL programs are used, plus a few more. When a company contracts with a third party for an online webinar, the third party commits to registrations for the event that are fulfilled either prior to the event or, if the agreement allows, after the event for people who watch the event recording. Understanding the success of filling webinar seats at the time of the event is a key metric as this not only shows the ability of the third-party media company to get registrations, but also provides some indication of the interest level in the general market for the topic. The second metric involves the number of attendees at the event as a percentage of total registrations. Higher- or lower-than-average drop-off of people from registration to attendance should be investigated. Understanding the initial rep disposition of the leads passed to sales is also an important metric that will be discussed in later chapters.

For online seminars that are managed exclusively in-house, the number of net new names registering for the seminar is a good metric, along with total overall registration, percentage attending, and lead disposition rates.

Finally, for both types of webinars, tracking engagement during the event is a good indicator of how interested the attendees were in the material. Attendance numbers during an online webinar can vary widely as people come and go. A truly engaging event will build attendance numbers during the event that peak somewhere towards the end. A not-so-engaging event will have numbers that peak early and gradually fall as people lose interest and drop off the call. Tracking the maximum number of attendees during the event as well as the point in time at which the max was reached is the metric for engagement. One note of caution here: Different webinar platforms use different types of underlying technology to deliver the webinar experience. Such differences in technology can create different measurement systems, so comparing engagement numbers between webinars that use different technology may not be as meaningful.

Offline trade shows and events can be a critical part of a B2B strategy. Effectiveness at offline events starts with getting badge scans of attendees and ultimately ends with website traffic driven by follow-up trade show offers. For a homogenous event at which everyone could be a prospect, the goal would be to get 100% of the attendees scanned. Of course few events contain 100% possible prospects, and simple physical layout and foot traffic constraints make it difficult to get a high percentage of visitors through a booth. In addition, the condition upon which badge scanning is done is critical to understanding the quality of a lead. Many B2B booths employ techniques for lead collection such as tee-shirt giveaways that may maximize badge scans but have little to do with actually engaging a prospect in a solution-selling discussion.

Still, taking the number of show attendees and dividing into that number the number of badge swipes can produce a good indication of the effectiveness of getting people to the booth at a show. This effectiveness is driven by booth location, size, and the efforts of booth staff in talking to people.

While collecting badge scans is good, collecting some form of additional information in the form of notes or a lead grade is even more critical, especially in situations in which the sales team will be asked to follow up with trade show booth attendees. Basic booth notes or grades to simply disqualify a prospect are critical. For example, if a company uses a four-call follow-up process for trade show swipes and 20% of the swipes can be disqualified at the show through a quick conversation, for a 1,000-swipe show 20% or 200 initial phone calls don't have to be made. Assuming the average call cycle is about three calls, the disqualification would mean that an additional 400 follow-up phone calls could be avoided. For a 100-call-per-day sales organization, that equates to six days of work eliminated simply by doing some on-floor qualification. For this and other reasons, measuring on-site information collection is important for physical trade shows.

Mystery Traffic

Prior to a weekly metrics meeting, the team member responsible for referring site traffic noticed a 30%+ increase in traffic over the previous week. There was no easy explanation for the increase as the traffic came from around the world and appeared to be hitting some random pages. The referring site domain names were not easily recognizable and the traffic had a 100% bounce rate. At the metrics meeting, the webmaster piped up. "Oh yeah, I turned on remote site monitoring. I wonder if that is now impacting referring site traffic." The answer, of course, was that it was. The web analytics package had started tracking the page requests from the site-monitoring provider. Some tweaking to the analytics package and some additional configuration changes to the site-monitoring software enabled the traffic to be excluded from analysis. But the example showcased the need for weekly discussions of metrics and the need to understand baseline traffic numbers so when something is out of spec, the team can quickly and easily understand why.

Take Action

The first step in the measurement process is to understand traffic and the resulting goal conversions. Ultimately, of course, marketers want to know if this traffic generates opportunities and whether these opportunities close. In later chapters we will look at how to measure the opportunity creation rates or lead disposition rates from these sources. But a solid understanding of traffic by source is the critical first step. Before moving on, consider doing the following:

- For each source above, log into Google Analytics and investigate the source in detail.
- Find out the person in your organization who is responsible for the actions that drive traffic for each of these sources.
- Do a deep dive into any paid spending. How much is being spent? On what types of programs?
- For PPM programs, investigate click rates in order to convert PPM spending to PPC spending.
- For PPC spending, investigate how many of the clicks convert to a lead to determine PPL spending levels. Now all three programs can be compared on their cost to generate a lead.

- Get familiar with conversion rates on the website by program. There are no right or wrong answers, just familiarize yourself with the results.
- Download the companion metrics sheet from www.storymetrix.com/resources if you haven't done so already, and implement the inbound traffic and paid traffic metrics.

Chapter 5: Measuring Website Goal Conversions

What You Will Learn

- Why tracking website goal conversions are important
- How to interpret form conversion rates
- Bouncing and exit rates overview
- A/B test overview

Overview

In the last chapter we looked at goal conversion rates by traffic source. The assumption was that, given a standard design, color template, form layout, or other site structure criteria, differing goal conversion rates by traffic source would be an indicator of traffic quality. In this chapter, we look at the entire website as a single goal converter and put in place measurement systems to improve its ability to hit goal conversions regardless of the source.

Examining goal conversions in aggregate across the entire site is important for another reason. From a marketing accountability standpoint, some marketers will be off trying to attract inbound traffic, others may be running PPC programs. Their job is to get traffic to the site and present compelling offers in order to hit goal conversions. But they don't have control over all aspects of this task. The site layout, design, colors, page rendering performance, and overall content flow (among other areas) are generally the domain of a web team. So while these other teams can drive quality traffic and present compelling offers, without the web team aligning on goal conversion as a whole, the overall conversion rates will suffer regardless of the quality of traffic or offers.

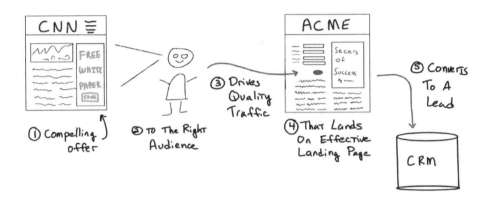

Figure 19: Compelling offers placed in front of the right audience should drive high click-through of quality traffic that hits a landing page and converts.

Much of the discussion on goal conversion will focus on the website. It is not clear, however, if this will remain the primary point of interaction over time. Social communities like Facebook and LinkedIn have other mechanisms to measure user engagement such as "Likes". Mobile applications also present non-web engagement models. Either way, goals need to be set and some method for measuring conversion established along with sub-metrics to track.

All marketing teams can tell depressing stories about group website design and decisions. At smaller companies, many times the CEO will get involved. At larger companies, an email from the CMO may suddenly alter the structure and design of the site. Throw in legal, the brand team, sales operations and maybe even support, and it is possible that a whole lot of people are weighing in on the site without having accountability for goal conversion. During the integration of one of my employers into a larger company, we noticed that what used to take three clicks for a goal conversion suddenly took six clicks on the parent company site. We were told that multiple groups had weighed in on how they needed the process to work. The result was a 50% reduction in goal conversion. Without a single team responsible for overall site goal conversion, site-wide design decisions can get made by committee with a less-than-optimal result for goal conversion rates.

Measuring Goal Conversion Rates

Measuring goal conversion rates is important as you strive to understand how effective the online site moves prospects through the sales funnel. A conversion occurs when a prospect takes an action that results in advancement through the sales cycle. A conversion could involve completing a form or watching a product video or even visiting a set number of product pages on a site. Setting conversion goals is critical to measuring the success of the website at moving a prospect through the sales cycle. A conversion rate would generally be expressed as a percentage of site visitors who complete a specific action. In Google Analytics, these are generally referred to as goals.

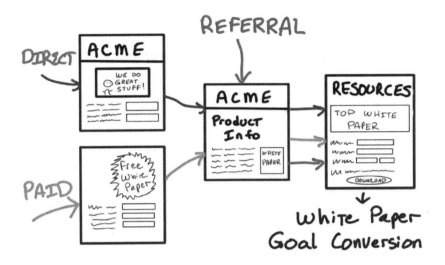

Figure 202: A goal that tracks white paper downloads would track the number of form completions divided by site traffic by source.

Many events happen on the way to a goal that can conspire to lower conversion rates. Visitors hit the site from top or side, don't like what they see, and immediately bounce. Perhaps visitors start traveling though the site, grow weary at the pace of content presentation, and exit on a page prior to an offer. Perhaps visitors make their way to an offer and determine that whatever they're being asked to do in order to get the offer is too onerous. Forms that require too many fields may demand too much from a prospect too soon. All these factors influence overall site conversion rates. Perhaps a prospect gets to a form, but fails to complete it. There are many such leakage points on a site from entry to goal conversion. The key is to plug the leaks.

While measuring the overall site conversion rate is an interesting exercise, it is not necessarily insightful into the strength of a site as a conversion mechanism, unless it is measured over a very long period of time with generally consistent traffic sources and offers of similar strength. As we have seen multiple times, traffic quality can dramatically skew conversion rates as well as offer quality. Poor-quality traffic won't convert and will lower site conversion rates. Poor-quality offers won't convert and will also lower site conversion rates. We have discussed the subject of quality traffic before. Now, let's look at offers.

Since a website is designed to achieve goal conversions, and since website visitors will show up at various stages of the sales cycle, most sites will have an early-stage offer, a mid-stage offer, and a late-stage sales cycle offer. Tracking conversion rates on each of these offers is important.

An early-stage offer could be a white paper. A mid-stage offer could be a product demonstration or a one-on-one call with an engineer. A late-stage offer may involve getting a quote or contacting sales. Even earlier-stage offers could require a prospect to simply view enough site content to appear interested in the company's offerings. Regardless, each offer will have different conversion rates, and understanding these rates is critical when making investment decisions. The key is to align the right offer with the right traffic source. A prospect who is immediately presented with an offer for conversion after arriving from a paid advertisement that said "Download a Free White Paper" will trust the website at a different level and react to such an offer differently than a prospect who has organically arrived on the website, traveled around, and decided to move forward in some manner.

Like many measurements, weekly site conversion tracking may not yield much value if the intention is to score the site based on conversion values. In fact, conversion rates for a site will probably change weekly based on traffic sources and offers. The real key is whether the marketing team can explain a given change week over week. Over time and with enough diversity in marketing programs and sufficient traffic, quarterly and annual site conversion averages will emerge to reflect the site's ability to convert traffic and the marketing team's ability to attract qualified prospects and place compelling offers in front of them. Given all these factors, it is not difficult to conclude that improving conversion rate can be challenging.

No Easy Answers

Like many parts of the B2B marketing challenge, there are no easy answers to improving site conversion. Impacting site conversion requires you to get inside the head of a site visitor, experience what a prospect experiences, and make a judgment about whether the information presented would cause someone to take the next step in the sales cycle. Understanding traffic flows to the site and within the site is also important. While much emphasis is put on a site's homepage, a majority of site traffic will come in through the sides of the site. Such traffic is comprised of search traffic to pages indexed deep inside the site, pay-per-click traffic going to landing pages, or email marketing traffic once again going to specific landing pages inside the site. The complexity of the traffic flows, offers, and multiple points of entry to the site makes it necessary for conversion improvements to include a combination of left-brain site design work and right-brain metrics analysis.

The design of forms on a website also directly impact conversions. Ask for too much information at the wrong time, and conversion rates will plummet. Top pages with exits represent another area to study, since they, too, represent leakage from the site. Unless a prospect leaves the site after completing a goal conversion, exiting the site anywhere represents leakage. Plugging these leaks should assist with site conversion. Pages with high bounce rates are similar to pages with high exit rates except that, in this case, prospects simply hit the page, then leave without diving deeper into the site. When considering the science of conversion, there are three places to look: high bounce pages, high exit rate pages, and form conversion rates. Examining flows inside the site is useful, but provides less of a roadmap for action.

"Too Much Orange"

The home page tends to get way too much attention from senior management on a website. It is not uncommon to get feedback from very senior members of the company about not liking "all that orange" or "that graphic". Such comments can churn a marketing team's time and resources without dramatically impacting the site's success. Most people fail to recognize that the home page is just not as important as CEOs and others may make it out to be.

The home page is important as the first impression someone will have of the company if they come through the front door of the site. If an investor or board member or potential acquirer wants to check a company out, they are going to start at the home page. However, in terms of B2B lead generation, much of the most qualified traffic will actually come in through the sides of the site since search engine terms often point to pages deep inside websites. The same goes for referring site traffic from key influencer sites that may point to specific blog postings or videos or interesting content deep in the site.

So while the home page on its own is the probably the number one landing page for a site, it may only represent 30% of the site's total landing page traffic. The other 70% of landing page traffic is scattered throughout a site. While paying attention to the home page is important, it is equally as important to understand what other landing pages are responsible for traffic.

Minimizing Bouncing

The first step in improving conversion rates is to make sure people who arrive at the website don't just drop off and leave. Some of this is inevitable and, as in all analysis, looking at bounce rates should involve breaking it down by traffic channel. With direct traffic, which involves people coming directly to a site based on their own navigation, one would expect a low bounce rate. Compare this to traffic generated by pay-per-click advertising, however. Very creative ads that get people to click may drive the wrong type of prospect to a site. Many pay-per-click ads also drive people to forms, which already have a high bounce rate. Add some poor-quality traffic created by an ad that draws the wrong prospects, and you've got a recipe for very high bounce rates.

Week over week, bounce rates by channel should generally remain stable. Dramatic differences either mean the traffic quality has suddenly changed, or the traffic that is arriving at the site is suddenly hitting a page that does not match prospect expectations. Deeper analysis of bounce rates can be performed by looking at top bounce rate pages by traffic source, and even getting more granular by looking at the referring URL to understand the concept of the referral. In many cases, site content may not be easily modified to improve the bounce rate. In other cases, pages can and should be modified, especially if they are landing pages, blog posts, or other unique pages that can be easily changed without impacting the entire site experience.

High Tuesday Bounce Rates

Tuesday bounce rates for direct traffic to a client site were higher than bounce rates on other days of the week. The trend was predictable. Upon further investigation, we realized that bounce rates went up on days on which the client sent out a weekly email blast. But this didn't explain the increased bounce rate, since the traffic source for these bounces was direct, not email marketing. Instead, it turned out, the large email blasts were driving people who saw the email had arrived in their inbox to go directly to the website rather than click a link in the email. If they did not immediately see something new or connected to the email they'd received, they bounced off the home page. To solve the problem, the home page was redesigned to include an email marketing tile that matched the particular email offer in a given week.

Examining bounce rates by channel provides a good top-level view of the site that should be checked on a weekly basis. A more thorough review, however, is required in order to reduce overall site bounce rates. Understanding and ranking the top bouncing pages each month and working to reduce the rates for these pages is a meaningful exercise. Removing from the analysis obvious high bounce rates covered by other programs like pay-per-click landing pages, email marketing pages, and other direct converting pages should leave a good selection of high bounce rate pages driven by organic traffic and direct traffic.

If referring site traffic is consistently hitting a blog post, for example, and bouncing, can the blog post be modified to be more topical? Is there some kind of offer that can be placed on the blog page to entice a reader to go deeper into the site or take some action? These are the types of decisions and analysis that should be undertaken in order to reduce bounce rates for traffic flow.

Getting Comfortable with Exit Rates

Analyzing bounce rates is a good way to understand when traffic hits the site and leaves without action. But where exactly does traffic leave the site? Some pages, such as the page that appears after a form is submitted, are logical exit points. Other pages, however, represent points at which traffic drops from the site because of a loss of interest. As with high bounce rate pages, examining exit rate pages represents another useful type of analysis.

High exit rate pages are assumed to be places where one would not normally expect people to depart the site. A high exit rate on a "thank you" page that pops up after a completed form is submitted is not necessarily a bad thing. Similarly, landing pages will not only have a high bounce rate, but will also have a high exit rate. People must leave a site somewhere. The question is, are they leaving the site on a page that makes sense to exit, or do particular pages have a higher exit rate than others?

Understanding the overall site average for exit rates for non-landing pages can provide a good idea of what the rate is for a site. For example, if the average exit rate of all pages that deal with product information is 45%, but one particular page spikes at 75%, something is probably wrong. Examining page design and site traffic flows and taking the user's point of view on page expectations might reveal why the page is especially leaky for traffic. Of course the reason for exiting the site may have nothing to do with the marketing story, and could actually be a product feature problem. If users are looking for a specific product feature that is absent, at some point — perhaps on the products and features page — the missing feature could cause an exit.

Measuring Conversion Paths

In addition to preventing prospects from bouncing right off the site, and working to make sure they exit the site at appropriate places, the next area for marketing executives to consider is how prospects flow through the site. This represents perhaps the most difficult aspect of improving site conversion rates and starts to solidly cross the line from science to art.

Many analytics applications provide visualizations to enable web teams to understand key traffic flows. The challenge is to boil this information down into a metric that provides value for senior managers on a recurring basis. The other challenge involves defining what is considered a "good" conversion path. Does high page count mean someone is more engaged, or just lost on the site? If the purpose of the site is to get people to download a white paper, does the fact visitors spend a long time on the site imply a better site visit than short time on the site if the end result is the white paper? In order to determine the ideal conversion path of a website, it is important to understand all of the site's goals.

One could assume that more site engagement is better as it represents someone accelerating down the sales cycle to learn about a product. But if too much information is presented, and the goal of the site is to get someone to take a phone call from sales or respond to an email, the site may actually not be effective. To resolve this issue, the art comes in. A website is a virtual trade show. If you were working at a trade show and wanted to engage someone, what would you do to attract them to talk to you? Once they're engaged and talking with you, what information would you be required to discuss to make this prospect ready to talk to sales? If such information is mapped out on the site as the "path" an ideal prospect travels, then the page count and flows can be used to create the ideal yardstick for how someone flows through the site. Comparing actual traffic flows to the ideal flow on a monthly basis would provide a good measure of how well the site is mapping to that physical trade show conversation. These ideal flows could be defined as a collection of pages and a measurement of the percentage of people who enter the page sequence and ultimately exit it at the goal.

Improving Form Conversion Rates

While optimizing traffic flows through a website can represent somewhat of an art form, form conversion rates are pretty straightforward to track and improve. If 100 prospects click to take an action and the action requires the completion of a form, measuring how many of those 100 prospects complete the form is a critical measure of goal conversion. The offer presented plus the form design contribute to the successful completion of the form. Of course the quality of the traffic also impacts form conversion rates, as does the form's position on the website. Forms that are integrated with a landing page will have lower conversion rates than forms that require the prospect to navigate the site, learn about products and solutions, then ultimately select some action. In the latter case, the prospect is significantly more committed to taking action than someone who simply responded to a website ad. For this reason, form conversion rates by traffic source represent an important part of the analysis.

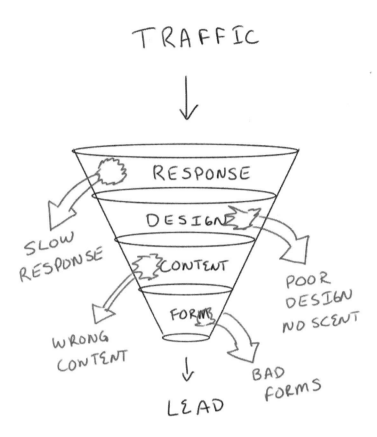

Figure 21: All traffic lands somewhere on a site and a percentage will convert to a goal. Site design, content, form fields, and form design all conspire to lower conversion rates and cause traffic to leak.

There are two specific measures for form conversion. The first is the overall conversion rate for the form. The second is the form abandonment rate. Form abandonment tracks the percentage of people who start filling out a form only to abandon the form prior to completing it. Form abandonment could occur due to technical issues with the form, the length of the form, or other problems.

On a weekly basis, form conversion and abandonment are critical percentages to track. Sudden decreases in form completion rates could be due to traffic, but could also be caused by system problems. Tracking form completion rates also provides a back-of-the-envelope number for the number of leads delivered by the website in a given day. This number should be cross-referenced with the data coming out of the CRM system to validate that the systems are operating correctly and passing data. This step is especially important when the CRM system is fronted with a marketing automation system.

Experimenting with form structure, layout, and surrounding text is perhaps the primary way to improve overall site conversion. While too much emphasis gets placed on website colors or graphics, too little attention is paid to the mundane world of form completions. Yet minor changes to a form can have a dramatic impact on overall site conversion rates in a perceptible manner. Much more than, say, changing home page colors or font sizes or adding links to specific pages.

Tracking Continuous Site Improvement with A/B Testing

While much of the website conversion work is artistic and not scientific, and much of the metrics don't reveal meaningful change on a weekly basis, there is one metric that is critical to track – the amount and scope of A/B testing underway and the convergence percentages for these tests.

The only way to improve overall site conversion rate in a methodical fashion is through consistent and ongoing A/B testing. Since improvements to site conversion only happen in small increments and require a significant amount of traffic for the tests to converge on an answer, making sure there are always A/B tests underway is critical to slowly but surely improving conversion efficiency.

A/B tests could check:

- Two different forms
- Two different product pages to see if one particular page has a lower exit rate than another
- Various offers, content, or images that could be added to a blog post in order to reduce bounce rates

To maintain the focus on A/B testing as something important to the entire organization, the names of the top A/B tests reaching convergence should be monitored as they approach statistical significance. Most of the A/B test algorithms provide some measure of certainty to their results. When results are determined, they should be shared as part of the ongoing metrics process.

Take Action

Conversion is one of the most vexing issues to track and improve. The multiple variables that impact conversion – traffic quality, offer quality, and site mechanics – make improvements difficult to implement. By focusing on pages with high bounce rates and exit rates, marketers can keep more traffic contained on the site. Then, by optimizing forms and other conversion mechanisms, overall conversion rates can be improved. Since conversion is a complex process, the key is to ensure the organization is constantly running A/B tests to gradually improve site conversions.

Next steps:

- Make sure goals are set up in analytics to track overall site conversion.
- Examine goal conversion rates by source.
- Identify high bounce rate pages and prioritize for repair.
- Identify high exit rate pages and prioritize high-leakage pages for repair.
- Determine form conversion rates and fix pages with poor conversion statistics.
- Standardize on a form design that drives the highest conversion.
- Download the companion metrics sheet from www.storymetrix.com/resources if you haven't done so already and implement the site goal conversion metrics.

Chapter 6: Nurturing

What You Will Learn

- Nurture segmentation and why it is important
- Using scoring to identify ripe leads
- Measuring database size and net new names and what it can tell you about your future customer acquisition

Overview

With successful goal conversion, prospects are entered into a nurture process to move them forward in the sales cycle so they are ready to engage with the sales team. Nurturing will take place in a variety of situations. In some cases, the returning prospects will restart a sales cycle. In other cases, fresh prospects may come to the site and rocket through the sales cycle steps and be ready to engage with sales after one session. In all cases, the key is to nurture prospects as far down the sales cycle as possible and deliver to the sales team sales-ready leads.

What is considered a sales-ready lead will vary by organization. There are multiple consulting firms, books, and strategies that describe what should be provided to a sales team. Ultimately, whatever is provided represents a best-guess estimate on a prospect's sales cycle position. A majority of leads that come in from the website and other sources, and a majority of the leads provided to sales, will be sent back to marketing to nurture. The key, therefore, is to implement a nurturing process that moves prospects through the sales cycle in an orderly manner.

Segmenting the Nurturing Process

As discussed in earlier chapters, defining a sales process is key for a variety of reasons, one of which is for nurturing. Theoretically, different nurturing offers will have different levels of effectiveness, depending on the prospect's stage in the buying process. An early-stage prospect who is still educating himself on the solutions available will probably respond poorly to an offer for a 25% reduction in the cost of a product. Conversely, a prospect that is ready to buy may get derailed in the buying process with a white paper that causes her to re-examine her purchasing requirements.

Hence, making an educated guess at exactly where a prospect stands in the buying process is important to correctly match their process stage with the various nurturing offers. How can you tell where a prospect is in the sales cycle for nurturing? Marketing gets a variety of indicators that provide less-than-definitive answers, but at least they offer a starting point for analysis. Indicators of nurture status include:

- Visiting pricing pages on the website
- Downloading product data sheets
- Engaging in online chat with a product specialist
- Long, in-depth conversations at a trade show
- Working with a sales rep
- Hitting the "Request a Quote" button
- Looking at numerous product specification pages on the website

Using these actions as indicators of customer interest, the marketing team can construct a model that places each prospect in a proper nurture bucket. Different offers can then be targeted to each bucket to move prospects down the sales cycle. Providing sales input into marketing's guess of the prospect's sales cycle stage is important so they can assist in tuning and potentially even turning off the marketing nurture processes.

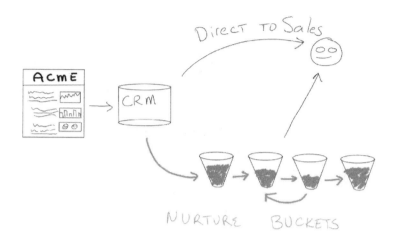

Figure 22: Some leads go directly to sales. Others must be nurtured through a four-step process that results in a percentage of nurture leads eventually going to sales.

With each prospect in the database assigned a stage in the buying process, it becomes possible to tally up the entire database by process stage and report on the number of prospects in each of the buying stages over time. If the far left-hand side of the database contains inactive prospects, and the far right includes prospects getting ready to purchase, then hopefully each week more and more people move left to right through the different stages while the total database size of active prospects increases. In fact, if done correctly, the size of each of the stages can provide a useful predictor for future sales revenue.

In addition to tracking the size of each of the nurture buckets, tracking how long prospects are inactive is also important. The amount of time that needs to pass before a prospect is deemed inactive will vary by company sales model. Inactive prospects can get activated and start moving through the sales process. However, as time goes on and a prospect's inactivity increases, the response rates for these leads will drop dramatically. Hence at some point, prospects need to be moved from inactive to a state in which they are rarely, if at all, marketed to. Otherwise, as time goes on and the database size increases, marketers will get a false sense of security from the ever-increasing numbers. The total size of the active prospect base is important, as is the size of the inactive prospect base within a reasonable time frame. But if database size reporting includes prospects that are years old and have taken no action, it will likely result in an overly optimistic accounting method for database size.

Old Prospects Don't Respond, They Just Fade Away

Over time we had built up a sizeable database of prospects through our inbound marketing efforts. A key category was the "inactive" segment, where prospects were moved if they took no action with the company over a 60-day period and were not associated with a sales opportunity. The inactive segment generally provided poor click-through rates on emails, but this was expected since the category was inactive. After two years of building the database, we went back and performed some analysis of the inactive group. What we found was that any of the click-throughs that were occurring were happening from the recently inactive prospects. Prospects without responses for 12 months rarely, if ever, responded. Clearly a different strategy was needed to revive these long-inactive prospects.

Using Scoring to Determine When a Lead is Ripe

One of the more challenging jobs for the marketing team is to make an accurate assessment of sales cycle location for a prospect. At some point, marketing has to objectively determine a lead is ready for the sales team. In addition to this key decision point, the marketing team also needs to decide the sales cycle location of a pre-sales prospect since, as we discussed before, the key is to send or market the right offers at the right times to these prospects. Accurately determining the stage at which a prospect resides is challenging enough via face-to-face-to-phone contact. Attempting to do this simply by observing behavior is even more challenging.

One solution that teams use involves calling all potential prospects and determining interest levels using a telemarketing team. While this approach is interesting, it does not provide sufficient objectivity and scale. If the lead qualification team is goaled on delivering qualified leads, this makes it especially difficult to achieve objective, repeatable results.

Another solution is to use website behavior as an indication of interest level. Most likely someone who spends a significant amount of page views on the site and then clicks "Contact Sales" is qualified for the sales team at the extreme. But what about someone who appears on the site, grabs a white paper, and returns in 30 days to click through some more product pages? Qualified for sales? If not qualified for sales, in what stage of the buying cycle is such a prospect located?

When site behavior is studied in this manner, a company can come up with a reasonable definition of which pages represent what level of interest for a prospect. A prospect downloading a white paper and then spending significant time on the careers page is probably not a hot prospect. Same for a prospect that stops by to read the blog and then exits the site. It should be possible for the team to develop a profile that the sales team agrees represents the online behavior a qualified prospect would exhibit. In a case in which a prospect is not qualified, the team also needs to agree on the mapping of resultant online behavior and its placement in a certain stage of the sales cycle.

This online mapping of behavior must be simple enough so that sales and marketers can quickly deduce why a lead was classified the way it was. Many marketing automation systems now have the ability to score leads as an objective way to identify sales-ready prospects. Lead scoring is one of the most critical measurement techniques for B2B marketers.

Lead scoring operates by assigning a numeric value to any number of events or attributes associated with a lead. The sum of these numeric values represents the score of the prospect. Theoretically, the higher the score, the further along a lead is in the sales process. When the score reaches a predefined value, the lead is determined to be sales ready. Scores can be reset below the sales-ready value if there is insufficient activity with the prospect over a set period of time.

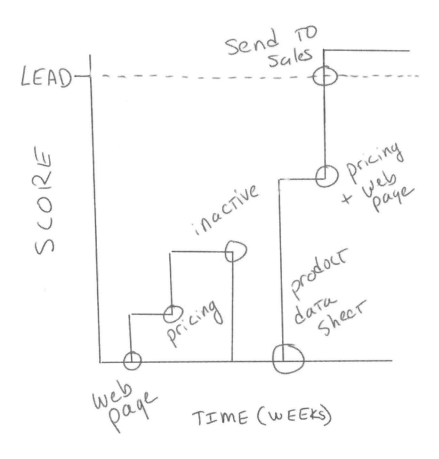

Figure 23: Scoring based on actions taken includes no action (inactivity) in order to produce a sales-ready lead.

A lifetime score for the prospect is also another interesting value to track. Theoretically, over time, the number of interactions a prospect has with the company should continue to go up. If website statistics, among other scoring values, are part of the scoring algorithms, the lifetime score of a prospect should continue to climb and provide an accurate predictor of sales stage. Scoring as a measurement of effectiveness requires a significant amount of communication and feedback from sales, in addition to statistical measurements of leads provided to sales.

Old-school marketing systems attempt to measure effectiveness by the numbers of white paper responses generated, or the number of booth attendees whose badges were swiped. This type of B2B measurement is important within the context of a particular program. If you attend a trade show and get a few badge swipes, it is unlikely the event will be considered successful. But sales doesn't operate at the program or campaign level. Sales is looking for marketing to identify in a holistic manner prospects who are far down the sales cycle. Scoring provides a way to pass along to sales prospects with profiles of activities and demographics that make them quality candidates.

There are several key measurements for scoring. The first is roughly the number of sales prospects each week that cross the scoring threshold. This is the absolute number of sales-ready leads that are passed to sales. The second metric involves understanding what percentage of these leads passed to sales are completely new to the sales team.

The third key metric for scoring is to understand the collection of actions that caused a prospect to trip the scoring threshold and be sent to sales. Scoring represents a collection of actions. No single action can represent the cause for a lead to move to sales since, in general, no single action can cause the threshold to be reached. Determining similarities among the multiple actions that cause leads to pass to sales (and hopefully create opportunities) can start to paint a statistical picture of what actions prospects go through to be sales ready. It also can provide a statistical rationale for setting scoring for individual actions.

When we initially stood up our scoring algorithm, the sales team had already been using a product called LeadLander which provided them a daily report of web traffic to the site by company name as resolved by IP address. The report also showed the web pages the prospect clicked on. Our sales team got savvy reading the web pages, which was great. But if a prospect came in from GM, for example, they couldn't tell who it was since LeadLander was just resolving IP addresses. Based on where the prospect clicked and how many pages they looked at, many times the reps would expect to see a lead from GM in their queue. If they didn't, they would walk into the marketing room and ask our marketing automation system admin to track down the lead and send it to them. Our initial lead scoring system wasn't sending them the names of the people who had just passed though the website and had performed a series of actions that led the sales team to deem prospects worthy of phoning. So with a few quick modifications to our scoring system, these types of leads went to the sales team for immediate follow-up. This was a great example of allowing everyone to see data and make informed decisions on their own about the types of leads they wanted. It also illustrated how absolute edicts from sales leadership ("I don't want any leads of type x") are not helpful. Sales and marketing both understand the importance of prospects that have exhibited a specific behavior through a series of actions that is more complex than the performance of a single action.

Location Uncertainty – Not Just in the Sales Cycle

While knowing where the location of a prospect is in the sales cycle can be challenging, understanding the location of a submarine can be extremely complex. In the 1980s when I was onboard a sub, GPS was just getting deployed. Determining your location on the surface was never the problem since you had celestial navigation and something called LORAN-C or OMEGA, an early land-based radio navigation system. NAVSAT was a satellite-based system that was an early predecessor to GPS, but it was nowhere nearly as accurate or quick.

The challenge came when you submerged. Once beneath the surface, all modes of navigation disappeared. While you could use sonar to map the bottom of the ocean, sonar makes sound and could have alerted the Soviets to our position. So the boat would get a fix on the surface, submerge, then use gyroscopes housed in an inertial navigation system on the boat to determine how far from the last fix the boat had traveled. The gyroscopes would track the ship's movements up, down, left, and right and plot an approximate position through what is called dead reckoning. Essentially, if the inertial navigation system detected the boat had moved 10 knots for an hour on a course of 000T over the ground, then the inertial navigation system would predict the boat was 10NM north of the last fix.

Over time, the circle of uncertainty about the accuracy of where we were would expand. This circle of uncertainty would literally be drawn on the navigation chart and enlarged every hour. A large circle of uncertainty was not a problem unless you started to get close to land, or you started to get close to the boundaries of your operating box. So on a routine basis we would have to come shallow, stick up a mast, and get a fix. On a cruise in the early '90s our navigator got a hold of an early-model GPS. I'll never forget the day when we surfaced and, as I prepared to climb up the sail of the boat to main the surface watch in the top of the sail, he handed me a GPS antenna on a stick, some duct tape, and a long cable. "Attach this to the sail so we can use GPS while on the surface."

B2B navigation of the sales cycle has many similarities. After talking to a prospect in detail, a sales rep can fix that prospect's position in the sales cycle, at least to some extent. But with a prospect who never contacts sales or who goes silent for an extended period of time, identifying sales cycle location is more like making an educated guess. There is always a big circle of uncertainty around such a prospect's location.

Email Marketing

Email marketing is one of the prime mechanisms used for nurturing prospects. Effective measurement of an email marketing program is important, especially if it serves as the cornerstone for the nurturing effort. Email marketing is measured in the same way in which many other programs are measured. Emails are simply impressions and, as with all impressions, click-through rates are the measure that matters, followed by goal conversion rates on the site. Open rates are often used by marketers as evidence of brand impression, but this seems sketchy at best. If the goal of the email marketing program is to nurture prospects through the sales cycle, then prospects taking real steps that can be scored as evidence of movement through the funnel should be the goal for tracking success.

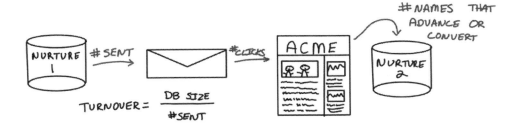

With prospects assigned to stages of the sales cycle, specific email marketing campaigns can be developed for each stage of the sales cycle. For example, prospects who are in the very early stage may be offered white papers on industry topics, whereas prospects who are in the late stage might not receive any email at all since, theoretically, they are already engaged with the sales team. While aggregate email marketing numbers are important to track, response and click-through rates by sales cycle stage are also important.

Some subjective market intelligence information can be gleaned from email marketing results as well. An expertly crafted email and offer that is just not compelling to the prospect audience can reveal much about what prospects want. This is especially true with white paper topics that are more thought leadership-oriented. Such considerations reside in the art side of campaign operations that complements the science of measurement.

Measuring Net New Names

Nurturing is a constant process of moving prospects towards sales engagements. But throughout the nurturing process, a percentage of prospects will completely disengage. This could occur due to:

- Prospects leaving companies and invalidating their contact info
- Prospects changing jobs within a company, removing them from the buying cycle for your product
- Losses to the competition that block your ability to sell to the prospect for a period of time
- Unsubscribes from your email campaigns
- Companies going out of business
- Prospects becoming customers

Growing the prospect database involves adding more prospect names through various marketing programs, both organic and paid. Understanding which programs add the most net new names at what cost is important from a marketing investment allocation perspective. Of course this must be augmented by ensuring that the new names entering the marketing process convert to sales-ready leads and, ultimately, opportunities.

While counting net new names is important, so is counting the percentage of net new names from a particular program. For some marketing channels, if you run the program long enough or return to the same physical events enough times, the same names will start coming in the funnel. Consider the effective size of your database compared to the number of potential prospects in the entire addressable market. Theoretically, even with a perfect database of all prospects, net new names would go to zero each week since all names would already be in the database. While theoretically possible, practically this is unlikely. But there is a relationship between market size and the percentage of new names a company can attract each week given the size of their database. Program exhaustion is critical to examine, both from a marketing spend standpoint and from a market size standpoint.

Trade Show Yields Drop

We attended the same trade show year after year with increasing booth size and square footage each year. The show was in a frothy market that was growing at 30% year over year total market size. However, the percentage of net new names from the show continued to drop year over year, which was surprising. While show attendance increased nearly 100% and our booth size increased, the number of net new names which had been as high as 85% gradually decreased to below 50%. We eventually concluded that a combination of repeat visitors to the show combined with marketing efforts through other channels was basically improving the quality of our database to the point that a given industry event only yielded 50% new names. The investment in these events continued despite the lower name yield, but the cost per new name increased dramatically.

Take Action

Nurturing is critical to getting leads to sales. In fact, a majority of leads will probably come through the nurturing process as opposed to going direct from a program to sales. For this reason, nurture measurement is critical to marketing effectiveness. One outcome of effective nurturing is sales-ready leads. Here is what you can do now:

- Determine your email turnover rate. This will provide an immediate indication as to how active the team is at sending emails and working the database.
- Talk with sales about the characteristics that make up a sales-ready lead.
- Calculate the size of your database. Calculate the number of contacts that have taken no action in the past year.
- Start tracking the weekly number of new names into your database and the weekly number of unsubscribes.
- Download the companion metrics sheet from www.storymetrix.com/resources if you have not done so already and implement the nurture metrics section.

Part III: Leads to Opportunities

Generated leads ultimately must become sales opportunities in order for marketing to be successful. Chapter 7 looks at measuring sales enablement. A sales team that isn't properly trained is unlikely to successfully generate opportunities. Measuring their skills on an ongoing basis is a critical part of the process. Chapter 8 and Chapter 9 then turn to the task of measuring opportunity creation. The problem for most B2B sales processes is that opportunity creation and closure can take months. Marketing can't wait months to see if their programs are working. To solve this challenge, Chapter 8 proposes a method of short-term opportunity tracking while Chapter 9 takes the long view. Both are important for assessing program effectiveness.

Chapter 7: Measuring Sales Enablement

What You Will Learn

- The three areas of sales enablement – reference materials, new-hire training, ongoing training
- How to measure each area
- Benefits of measuring, especially when working with sales leadership

Overview

Previous chapters mainly focused on measuring marketing's ability to generate and pass leads to the sales team. Traffic measures, conversion measures, and nurture statistics provide visibility into the operations of the lead machinery. But measuring marketing effectiveness also includes understanding how the sales team is enabled to follow up on leads passed to them. Leads must be passed to a sales team that is current in its training of products, competitors, and core sales plays. The sales team needs access to the core documents that govern how to handle objections, discovery, and account qualification and provide instructions on how to operate the many systems today's sales teams use to generate revenue for a company.

In addition, when a lead has been passed to the sales team, marketing's commitment to opportunity generation doesn't end there. At this point in the sales cycle, the sales team has taken over as the primary driver of the lead. Marketing, however, must still deliver email templates, call templates, case studies, and ROI documents, among other materials, in order to ensure effective conversations with the customer continue.

To support this sales enablement phase, marketing must measure two general areas of enablement:

- Reference material completion and the availability of marketing support materials for the late-stage sales cycle
- Training completion

All of this, if executed properly, will result in higher lead to opportunity conversion rates and higher opportunity to close rates. There is no single white paper or ROI document that will be "key", despite many anecdotal comments that insist something is the "key" to closing a deal. Success requires the combination of a well-trained sales team armed with the right reference material and supported by late-stage marketing efforts.

Not Our Problem

While working with a client on a sales to lead conversion model, the marketer on the project stated "We can't control what happens to leads when they get to ales". This type of "not my problem" approach ignores several factors that the marketer does control. The first is the quality of the leads. As we have reviewed, it is possible to game the system and deliver poor-quality leads that behave as though they are high quality by using low hurdle rates for lead generation and highly enticing offers that may drive significant numbers of very low-quality conversions. The other factor the marketer can control is the preparedness of the sales team to convert leads to opportunities. Training materials and training programs directly impact this. When quality leads are delivered to a well-trained sales team, opportunity conversion rates should normalize. Marketing can control this. This doesn't absolve the sales team from responsibility, but marketers need to be aware that the opportunity creation rate is a joint metric both teams need to own.

Measuring Reference Material Completion and Late-Stage Sales Cycle Material

The term "sales playbook" is generally used to describe the body of material the sales team references that contains everything from objection handling to order processing to competitive attacks. If this playbook is not current, it is impossible to consistently prepare training materials for new-hire classes or ongoing training during the course of the year, or to answer everyday questions in a repeatable way that helps ensure you only have to answer a question once.

Like all items in B2B marketing, measuring the completeness of this playbook is important for several reasons. First, identifying which sections are out of date helps to prioritize marketing's time and projects. Second, jointly agreeing with sales on which sections are less than complete or out of date helps prevent misunderstandings in which marketing thinks a section is current, but sales finds the material useless.

Developing and measuring playbook completeness is an art. Unless a market is very static, the sales playbook will never be current. Competitive changes, organizational learning, and new product announcements cause the playbook to be in a constant state of flux. Even in the case of a new playbook developed for a sales kick-off meeting, the playbook will be out of date by the end of the meeting due to discussions that occurred during the meeting around improving the current sales strategy.

Developing a measuring system for the sales playbook involves first determining which materials are required to support the sales cycle. For each step in the sales cycle, sales will require various types of documents such as:

- Elevator pitches
- Objection handling documents
- Call scripts
- Discovery questions
- Competitive one-pagers
- Product configuration information
- ROI discovery questions
- Customer case studies
- Compelling event definitions
- Sales cycle step definitions
- Specific solution plays
- Customer-ready presentations
- Business justification documents
- Product overview presentation
- Order processing instructions

This is just a sample of what may be required to operate a well-trained B2B sales force. At any given point in time, such documents could be nearly accurate to unusable. To measure document usability, assign a score based on the document's state. The exact number is not important as much as simply identifying which documents are out of specification and which are good enough. Since some topics have a higher importance than others, a scoring system should also be weighted. For example, without an agreed-upon set of discovery questions, having a thorough ROI analysis becomes less important since discovery is the first step in any sales engagement process. In this case, the discovery questions document might be more highly weighted than the ROI document.

The softer side of tracking sales material readiness is to interlock with sales leadership and agree upon both the state of the materials and priority to continuously bring new items up to speed. The readiness matrix provides a discussion guide that should be reviewed with sales leadership monthly in order to prioritize what has to occur next to keep the sales team operating. In addition, sales teams are always looking for new materials and angles to win deals. The readiness matrix provides a way to add new materials in an organized fashion, discard materials that are no longer in use, and — more importantly — provide a plan of record for what should be expected from marketing. The sales appetite for new materials is always greater than marketing's ability to deliver them, even in the best marketing organizations. A knowledge base readiness report provides a way to acknowledge what has already been provided, identify current gaps, and document what new materials need to be provided.

Providing a complete set of needed documents is a good starting point for sales enablement. Ideally, of course, you would also like the sales team to use these documents on a regular basis. For this reason the next step to measuring sales enablement involves determining if anyone is actually using the documents marketing is constantly producing and updating.

Depending on the method of publication of such documents, it could be possible to easily measure usage. Usage could be measured by tracking file downloads, page views of an intranet site, or views of a video. By measuring reference material usage item by item and also in aggregate, such documentation can provide the marketing team with valuable indicators of whether the sales team can access the material, finds the material useful, and is referring others to consume it. Measuring page views or visitors to a data store in aggregate is important. Measuring usage piece by piece is time consuming, but very useful when prioritizing which pieces of content to revise. Unused content that is considered to be highly valuable but is slightly out of date deserves deeper analysis. Is such content unused because the sales team actually does not find it valuable, or does the current state of such content prevent sales usage?

Do You Want to Buy?

You can hear everything in an open office. For a marketer tasked with sales enablement, such an office plan can allow you to sit near the sales team and overhear what they are saying to prospects. There are few ways to gain a better understanding of how well prepared or unprepared the sales team is to engage with prospects than by overhearing these conversations. Such conversations can also provide a source of inspiration to marketers for both new ideas and best practices.

One company I worked for sold software that users could first download and trial. One sales rep would literally call prospects with the greeting "You downloaded our software, would you like to purchase it?" No discovery, no relationship building, nothing. Just "Do you want to buy?" Needless to say this rep did not last long on the sales floor, and each time he called someone, everyone grimaced. His conversations provided motivation for the sales team to establish more stringent discovery questions that all reps were required to use. Open offices and close proximity between marketers and inside sales teams are invaluable for getting informal feedback from sales teams.

Scoring Training

Having all the field enablement documents current and up to date is one step for making sure the sales team is enabled. The next step is to structure training around the knowledge base and implement the training.

Training can be divided into two broad categories. The first is new-hire training for all new hires. The second category is ongoing training, which might include everything from a weekly webcast to an annual sales kick-off training event. Measuring training involves both tracking attendance and, more importantly, scoring knowledge retention.

New-Hire Training

Each new-hire training class provides the opportunity to review, the sales knowledge base and validate that it is accurate and up to date. If done correctly, each new-hire training class simply draws on material already present in the knowledge base. New-hire training then simply becomes a measure of who attended combined with scores on new-hire certification exams.

In addition to tracking completeness of training, tracking certification exam scores also provides data on how well new hires are absorbing the information they're given. Creating simple certification exams of multiple choice questions is an easy way to test the effectiveness of both training and retention.

Ongoing Training

While major sales kick-off events present an opportunity for additional training, the ability to hold remote meetings makes it easy to conduct training on a weekly basis as an ongoing part of any field enablement program. Given that the sales playbook is the collection of all information that the sales team should know, simply training once on the material at new-hire orientation or a sales kick-off is insufficient. Ongoing training is critical to keep the sales team fresh on all parts of the sales playbook. Properly constructing a sales training plan requires determining how frequently the team needs a refresher on each part of the sales playbook. Training on discovery questions, for example, should be completed perhaps once a quarter. A topic such as ROI analysis, on the other hand, may only require training every six months. Either way, a concise laid-out training plan that covers the entire sales playbook at least annually is important for measuring the success of ongoing training.

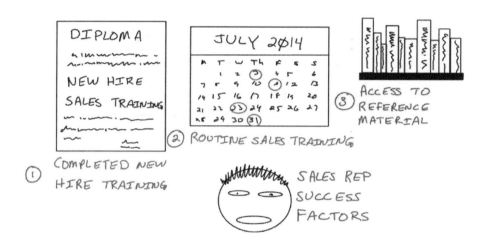

Figure 3: A trained sales team has access to a nearly complete reference library, has attended new-hire training, and regularly attends effective, ongoing training.

With the training plan developed, the key metric to track is actually post-training survey feedback from the sales team. Using any of the various survey systems, the sales team should be queried with a few simple questions that ask them to rate how strongly the delivered training will help develop and close more business. Another option is to use post-training exams from the same exam bank of questions used for new-hire training. Either way, some measure of post-training effectiveness needs to be conducted.

Keeping the RPMs Up to Date

Training was critical to a submarine's operations. Among the more critical documents on the boat were the reactor plant manuals, or RPMs. Calling them a document is a bit of an understatement. RPMs were actually a bookshelf-long series of manuals that contained all the operating instructions for how to start up, operate, and shut down the reactor. The RPMs also contained critical instructions for dealing with emergencies and other contingencies. The RPMs had to be up to date and current.

To help keep a ship's RPMs up to date, the RPMs were all registered. They were classified documents and each had a number. Second, each RPM had a change log in it. When a change was issued to the RPM, the engineering team was trained and tested on the change. Then the change was manually inked into the document and signed off by the person making the change. To ensure the change was done correctly, a second checker would often verify this.

The Navy would often send inspectors onto a boat to verify the RPMs were all accurate and all changes had been entered in correctly. If a major change was missing, this was a very serious incident since essentially the argument could be made that the crew was not operating the reactor in accordance with approved procedures.

That just sounds bad.

Luckily for the marketer, things are not so bad. But keeping the documents that explain how the sales team is supposed to operate current is slightly more challenging. Unlike submarine operations, which change infrequently, operating procedures for a sales team — especially one in a dynamic market — can change quite frequently. New competitors, new lead programs, new products all change the sales plays almost monthly. Staying current is often difficult, but essential.

Take Action
- Inventory sales reference materials currently used.
- Sit with sales and determine what is ideally needed to support the sales

cycle.

- Inventory the sales reference materials currently available.
- Grade all materials on a scale of completeness.
- Look at the new-hire training schedule. Does it teach the materials in the reference library?
- Investigate the frequency of ongoing sales training. Does ongoing training cover all the materials in the reference library at least annually? What does the training plan look like for the year?
- Download the companion metrics sheet from www.storymetrix.com/resources if you have not done so already and implement the sales effectiveness metrics.

Chapter 8: Short-Term Opportunity Effectiveness Tracking

What You Will Learn

- Importance of short-term opportunity measurement
- Sales compliance and follow-up metrics
- How to create a model for global dial capacity
- Importance of measuring sales support activity
- Importance of lead disposition tracking

Overview

With leads passed to an effectively trained sales team, the next step in the B2B measurement process involves short-term opportunity effectiveness tracking.

Why short term?

For most B2B opportunities, it can take months for leads to turn into closed deals. It can even take months for a lead to turn into an opportunity, depending on the criteria that the sales team uses for opportunity creation. Marketers in a high-volume B2B model can't wait that long to sit back and evaluate results. Online spending with ad networks, for example, can be modified daily if needed. But other marketing programs require 90 days of set-up to properly implement. Even ad networks can take months to increase spending and see results. Hence waiting to see long-term opportunity-closed results from a program that takes 90 days to implement means no correction to marketing spending would occur for six months to a year. Getting a quick snapshot of program effectiveness is therefore critical to continuing, adjusting, or canceling a program. This quick feedback loop, if done correctly, allows marketing organizations to shift to a more real-time process driven by short-term results. Measuring short-term effectiveness enables the marketing team to shorten the planning horizon for programs, and prevents semi-annual planning cycles that can take a significant amount of time to develop and are out of date by the time of implementation.

A couple of broad areas of measurement are used to track short-term effectiveness. First, to make any measurement effective, the sales team must follow up on leads quickly in a manner that supports the sales model. Second, the sales team must close out each lead when completed with a subjective disposition regarding the lead's worth. The subjectivity of such evaluations can be the source of significant angst to a marketing organization. However, with a great-enough sample size, sales reps who game the system with overly pessimistic lead dispositions or overly sunny results can be identified and their values adjusted.

Tracking Sales Follow-Up

Before evaluating the success of a particular stream of leads, the sales team needs to properly follow up on leads in a manner that is consistent with the marketing and sales model. If there is not adequate follow-up within a prescribed time frame via the correct process, then any measurement of the lead's value is immediately suspicious.

In broad terms, leads can be classified as open/untouched, in a state of being worked by the sales team, or in a state of completion. Within the category of being worked by the sales team, the sales organization may employ a multi-step call/email process. When leads are complete, they are evaluated for effectiveness for marketing. Key to all measurement is the ability to track, down to the rep level, the number of open leads and leads being worked on a daily, and sometimes hourly, basis depending on the operating model for the company. Done correctly, the sales follow-up report should show a waterfall of open leads at the top, followed by leads being worked, then finally leads closed out and completed.

At the senior management level, the number of open leads sitting in the queue every Monday morning can be recorded along with the number of leads being worked and the number of leads closed the prior week. Since this report represents a snapshot taken on a single day of the week, the only open leads should be those generated within the time frame that leads are allowed to be open. In other words, if leads are supposed to be followed up on within 24 hours, a snapshot report run Monday morning should only show new leads that arrived on Sunday.

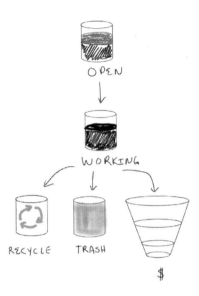

Figure 4: Leads should either be open, in some state of being worked, or closed. If closed, they should be recycled, junked, or placed into the sales funnel. Measuring the weekly size of each of these buckets is important.

From a senior management perspective, the waterfall chart showing the status of lead follow-up can be used to quickly pinpoint trouble spots where organizations are not receiving sufficient leads or where a major trade show or event has put too many leads into the sales process. In addition, tracking global lead status will also reveal uncovered territories or sudden changes in lead distribution by territory.

Peruvian Click Farms

A sudden increase in open leads in a generally quiet territory in Latin America was suspicious. An investigation revealed that a pay-per-click program was driving leads into this territory. A quick quality check of the leads showed extremely poor quality and settings in the AdWords program that should have disqualified this country. The PPC team had missed this anomaly because the data at aggregate from a PPC perspective was large enough to mask this problem. When cut by sales territory, however, the anomaly showed itself and was corrected.

Tracking Compliance

Getting a report on global lead status is useful for tracking overall flows through the lead processing system. Another key global measure that ultimately should be tied to individual sales reps is the percentage of leads outside of compliance for follow-up. If leads are supposed to be followed up within 24 hours, for example, worked for no more than 30 days, and then closed, the number of leads outside compliance on a global basis will highlight problematic regions, reps, and potential lead sources. When snapshots are taken on a periodic basis and the data is analyzed historically, tracking records of compliance can be established and potentially correlated with rep performance.

Figure 27: Over time, a familiar lead distribution should show up for each rep. In this case, Mary has nothing working, and everything closed. She is most likely gaming the system and just closing out leads.

Tracking System Capacity

In addition to looking at compliance, measuring the percentage of total call or email capacity consumed by leads in the system is also important. Assuming B2B efforts are consuming primarily inside sales rep call cycles, each rep generally has a goal for the number of calls to make each week. With this number established, the total capacity of outbound calls can be calculated by region and globally. Each inbound lead given to the sales organization contributes to the consumption of call cycles. If there is a four-step call process over four weeks, for example, and 100% of the leads have valid phone numbers and 100% of the prospects don't answer the phone or communicate in any way back to the rep, then for every 100 leads given to a rep, this would consume 400 call cycles over a four-week period. Of course some prospects pick up the phone and communicate, other leads may have bad phone numbers, leads may be connected to existing deals, or email may succeed in contacting the prospect. Building a model around the required effort for each lead placed on the sales floor is important so marketing can know if they are supposed to increase supply at a faster or slower pace to meet the capacity of the sales team.

New leads aren't the only things consuming outbound sales dials. During a given week, reps are also working existing deals in the pipeline. These deals are probably not associated with recently provided leads. Rather, these are deals from leads from months or weeks earlier that were already processed. In addition, the sales team may also be following up on leads from partners or from other sales teams inside a large corporation, or doing warm calling into old prospects in the database based on previous interactions. The number of available lead dials can be found, then, by taking total dial capacity and subtracting out the assumed number of dials to support existing opportunities as well as the number of prospecting dials the sales team will do on leads not generated by marketing.

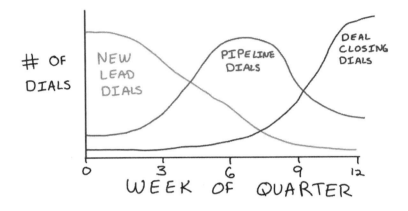

Figure 28: Available dials for calling new leads decreases as the quarter progresses and the urgency to close new business increases.

Understanding the capacity number is very important. Many sales and marketing teams will take revenue goals, divide by an average selling price, divide by opportunity close rate, divide by opportunity creation rate, and come up with a required lead volume for marketing. While theoretically this is correct, there are too many jumps and assumptions inherent in these calculations to make these numbers actionable. If sales doesn't have enough sales reps, it doesn't matter how many leads marketing supplies. If sales is spending time following up on leads from other sources that have better yields than some classes of marketing leads, then marketing should dial down the volume. If sales accelerates its rate of hiring new reps, marketing will need to keep pace.

The concept of matching marketing contribution to capacity as opposed to reverse-engineered revenue goals can be further explained with a factory analogy. If an automotive company wants to build and sell 10,000 trucks at about $10,000 each, the bumper supplier is asked to supply 20,000 bumpers, not "enough bumpers to make $100M in revenue". The revenue number is beyond the bumper supplier's control. But the target number of bumpers is not.

The key lies in not just delivering these bumpers, but in delivering them at the right time and place to keep the line running smoothly. In addition, over the course of a year, the auto plant may decide to change bumpers, add a supplier, or change production numbers. The bumper manufacturer needs to stay focused on keeping bumpers supplied to the weekly production numbers and let the manufacturer worry about the total output. If the bumper manufacturer delivers all 20,000 bumpers but in a lumpy fashion that slows down the production line, the bumper manufacturer will be fired.

It is the same with marketing. Understanding the available dial capacity and the number of leads marketing needs to fill is critical. Said another way, a VP of sales with call queues filled with quality leads that convert to opportunities at a known rate will be happy. It is the measure that is immediately in front of him each week that matters. The longer-term marketing lead to opportunity close figure is remote and not always easy to measure.

With the total sales capacity known, the next step is to calculate consumed capacity. The outbound call volume metric should be checked to see if it matches both the required dials for new leads and what is required to move leads currently in the funnel through the sales process in order to support existing opportunities. Most organizations use some manner of outbound call tracking for inside sales teams. By recording this data for each rep, comparing against the new leads for each rep, and then subtracting out the number of dials for opportunity follow-up, it is easy to determine whether sufficient follow-up is taking place.

Tracking Sales Support Activity

While tracking sales activity is insightful, more valuable information can be gained from tracking the activities of sales support personnel who assist the sales team in developing and closing business. For technology companies, many times this role is filled by a sales engineer who understands the technical aspects of a product. Some companies may use financial experts to develop financing and ROI models. Whatever this selling resource's function, tracking their utilization or engagement in the sales cycle can yield signification information.

For example, if sales must typically require a proof of concept that utilizes sales engineering, then forecasted opportunities in which the sales engineer has not indicated a completed proof of concept are suspect. Likewise, if the opportunity creation process generally requires a remote demonstration of the product, then extremely low utilization of the product demonstration team may indicate opportunities are being created without meeting the opportunity qualification criteria.

Sometimes sales resources are only supposed to be used at a particular stage of the sales process. For example, let's say the financial services team is supposed to be engaged at the proposal stage. By measuring the number of opportunities that entered the proposal stage and comparing this to the number of hours or engagements the financial services team accomplished during the corresponding period, it is possible to generally validate that the financial services team is being used at the correct point in the sales funnel. Engagement numbers that are too high may indicate that the financial services team is being used earlier in the sales cycle than planned. While this may not be bad, it serves as an indicator that the sales cycle as designed is operating differently than expected. If explored further, this provides an opportunity to modify, change, or adapt the sales cycle to the reality of how it is operating. The trick is to measure the usage, determine when it is off-track, then work to either return the usage back to normal with additional sales training or materials, or adjust staffing levels based on a revised sales model.

Closing Out Leads

Completing lead follow-up will result in a disposition. A lead may result in an opportunity, or it may involve bad data or lose its standing as a potential prospect for any number of other reasons. Sales teams must develop a concise list of disposition codes for use when leads are closed out. Assigning a disposition code represents the first subjective disposition of lead closure that is critical for the marketing team to use when designing marketing programs. The concept of closing out a lead is also important from a service level perspective. While sales reps can continually prospect into their accounts, a lead passed from marketing has theoretically reached a scoring threshold which should make it more susceptible to sales contact and engagement. After a period of time, a judgment call needs to be made on whether marketing's decision was correct. Most of the time (and in fact a vast majority of the time), marketing's scoring system will result in leads passed to sales that are not quite ready for follow-up. But marketing will never be able to tune their algorithms unless a definitive call is made by sales regarding the disposition of the lead they were passed.

Closing out a lead could happen on the same day the lead is passed to sales, or it could take the full length of the service level period. But by the end of the service level period, the sales team should be able to enter a disposition for a majority of the leads. Sample lead dispositions could be:

- No response
- New opportunity
- Existing opportunity
- Existing customer
- Not a corporate user
- Bad data
- Press or analyst
- Not qualified due to size, lack of pain, etc.

Each of these dispositions could assist marketing in making critical future investment decisions.

Over time, analysis of lead dispositions by program yields average values for items such as bad data, opportunity generation, etc. Deviation from these average values should cause either alarm or excitement within the marketing team. For example, bad data is a critical value to watch. Online advertising programs that rely on advertising networks are notorious for resulting in forms filled out with bad data. Some measure of bad data may be acceptable to these programs, but large deviations should raise alarms with the marketing team. Another example is a highly successful program that delivers high-quality names, even with correct titles, but the names are not qualified due to the company size or a lack of pain point. These leads may be interesting to nurture going forward, but may also indicate the need for a change in the marketing program.

Comparing all lead disposition rates across programs but also across sales reps can provide very valuable insights. While opportunity conversion rates are tough to compare between reps, items such as bad data should be equal across territories. The same factor is true for leads not qualified due to size or lack of pain.

Tracking disposition rates must be done in a systematic fashion. Attempting to look at weekly disposition rates is not necessarily useful since in a given week leads from various sources and programs and even time frames are getting final disposition codes. Measuring lead disposition should look at results for a given batch of leads provided to the sales team in a particular time frame from a particular program.

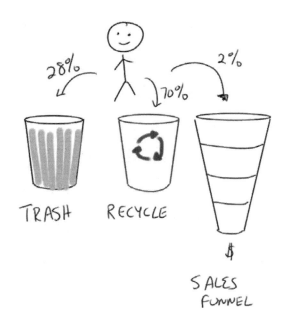

Figure 29: Sales reps are human sorters of leads. Eventually they toss leads into the opportunity funnel or the trash, or they recycle them.

At the most basic level, treating each month as a lead batch is one way to start to acquire useful data. All leads provided to the sales team in January, for example, would be tracked as a group or as a bucket of leads. In this case, if lead disposition is measured weekly for the January leads, there would be a significant number of open leads early on. The percentage of bad-data leads as a percentage of closed-out leads would also be very high. Leads with bad data are identified on the first touch so they appear quickly in lead disposition reports. No-response leads would be very low as a percentage since a 30-day call cycle would require that no-response leads not be tagged as such until February rolled around and the lead process was completed.

As January rolls into February, the bucket report for January would start to change in composition. More and more leads would get marked with no-response or other disposition codes. Opportunities would start to show up. Bad data would remain generally flat. As February rolls into March, the January leads would approach their final disposition codes and percentages. At this point, better measurement could be made on this batch of leads. Looking at January leads and going down one level would also provide information by program and disposition. This bucket report is one of the more critical reports for measuring first-pass effectiveness of both lead programs and sales rep follow-up.

Take Action

Short-term lead disposition tracking is critical to making course corrections and enhancing sales skill coaching. Ultimately, however, leads need to result in opportunities that are not only promising, but eventually close. Getting to this level of analysis is complex. The next chapter examines long-term program effectiveness tracking. But before tackling that, you can:

- Inventory short-term lead disposition classification.
- Determine what percentage of leads in a given month end up as opportunities.
- Look for differences in opportunity creation rates between reps.
- Generate a report showing compliance in order to establish lead follow-up processes.
- Create a model using available dials to determine maximum weekly lead flow to sales.
- Find reports showing the weekly dials by rep.
- Download the metrics tracking sheet www.storymetrix.com/resources if you have not done so already and implement the lead disposition and sales follow-up metrics.

Chapter 9: Long-Term Program Effectiveness - Campaign Level Reporting

What You Will Learn

- The various pitfalls to long-term campaign effectiveness tracking
- A more practical approach to campaign measurement
- Why funnel contribution and marketing contribution to revenue can skew program results

Overview

Short-term rep disposition reporting provides an immediate snapshot to the marketing team about the effectiveness of marketing programs. Tracking short-term opportunity creation rates from a particular program can provide a strong indicator of program success. However, most marketing organizations require that program analysis extends all the way to pipeline creation and closed deals. This end-to-end measurement is fraught with potential pitfalls. Still, using short-term program measurement combined with long-term influenced campaign tracking can provide a somewhat useful measure of long-term campaign effectiveness.

Pitfalls to Tracking Long-Term Campaign Effectiveness

The connection of closed or created deals to marketing programs should be simple enough. Leads passed to sales should contain campaign codes of the source program. However, in order for the program to be credited with the opportunity, the lead must be associated with the opportunity by the sales rep. Since the lead generally has program information attached to it, this should be easy. However, in some cases, the opportunity created may not actually involve the original lead. Rather, it may have come about through discussions with the original lead in which a referral was made to a new contact that originated the opportunity.

Other issues occur when attaching opportunities with programs. Depending on the complexity of the marketing programs, a single lead may have been targeted and may have responded to multiple programs. Some marketing organizations assign credit for the opportunity to the last program the lead responded to. This approach ignores the prior campaigns and, in the case of marketing organizations that utilize significant nurturing campaigns, will assign most campaign credit to nurturing. This would be inaccurate since there would have been no names to nurture without the original program in which the new names were identified.

Figure 30: Short-term lead tracking is easy since it simply measures what happens when a rep touches a lead. Long-term is more complex as the cycles start, stop, rewind, and change actors.

Calculating pipeline contribution also has pitfalls. A single large opportunity, for example, will distort a program's effectiveness. Spending $1M on a marketing program that yields a single $5M deal could appear successful from an ROI standpoint, but if the $1M only resulted in a .00001% opportunity creation rate, repeating the spend is unlikely to get the same repeat results.

Pipeline contribution can also under-report a program's success. Early-stage opportunity sizing by the sales team is almost always inaccurate. Experienced reps will undersize an opportunity until their confidence increases in both the opportunity's scope and certainty. Inexperienced reps will be overly optimistic and size an opportunity because they have ignored the impact of competitive pressures, budgets, and client negotiation skills. The result is a broad range of opportunity sizes that make ROI analysis very challenging.

Practical Method for Long-Term Program Effectiveness Tracking

A more practical and artful method of tracking program effectiveness that might require changes in the way marketing measures success needs to be used. Simple end-to-end campaign tracking is difficult, as is pipeline contribution tracking. But there is a way to track program effectiveness.

For a given program, the first checkpoint is the short-term opportunity creation disposition. If a marketing program generates net new names, there is a good chance that it is tapping into a new pile of potential prospects as long as its lead disposition rates are within the normal range compared to other programs.

Let's look at the disposition codes from two programs:

	A	B
# LEADS	100	100
TRASH LEADS	50%	20%
WRONG SIZE COMPANY	30%	10%
$ OPPS	2%	1%
NURTURE	10%	60%

From an opportunity creation standpoint only, program A appears to have been more effective with a 2% opportunity creation rate versus program B's 1%. However, in this case, the yield was only one more opportunity than program B based on the 100 leads. The vast majority of what arrived through program A will not be usable in the future. Fully 50% of the leads were bad data, another 30% came from prospects outside the target-size criteria for a prospect company, and another 8% were not even corporate users. Program B, however, yielded a significant cache of names to be nurtured, a smaller percentage of bad data names, and few non-corporate users. Program B should yield greater opportunities over time, especially if nurturing efforts at the company are successful.

Using pipeline contribution could further skew the analysis of which program was more effective. Program A discovered opportunities that totaled $1M and the single opportunity program B discovered was only $200,000, making program A look that much better. But it wasn't.

How are campaigns measured, then?

The first step involves recording the short-term sales rep disposition status and determining:

- Cost/Name
- Cost/Lead
- Opportunity creation rate
- Cost/Opportunity
- Bad data rate
- Non-corporate user rate

The next step is to record long-term campaign tracking results. Long-term campaign tracking should be performed well beyond the time requirement for sales to close out leads, and most likely beyond the average sales cycle. Looking back at campaign tracking too soon may make it difficult to effectively determine campaign success.

If a prospect visits a trade show booth and purchases in two years, should the trade show be credited with the opportunity? The answer is yes. Even in volume marketing, each marketing touchpoint contributes to the prior touchpoint's ability to drive new customers. Attempting to say that the last white paper downloaded made all the difference to create the opportunity ignores all the campaign work undertaken to get a prospect to the opportunity creation point.

For practical tracking purposes, however, the marketing team must decide on a time period for closing out campaign success tracking. The key is to identify those campaigns through which no deals have closed as opposed to trying to determine with great certainty the difference between two campaign opportunity creation rates. Let's assume that six months is the time horizon before a campaign is closed out. Within the first 30-60 days, early-stage rep disposition tracking should provide an indication of campaign results. At the six-month point, one can measure whether the lead with its attached campaign has been associated with an opportunity. If this is the case, then the number of opportunities associated with a campaign can be tallied.

Hence, in addition to the metrics above, the number of opportunities associated with a program should be calculated at the agreed-upon program close-out point.

Third-Party Media Buys

Long-term opportunity tracking is important to ensure marketers are not fooled by false indicators of good lead quality. A client was using extensive third-party media in the form of pay-per-lead programs that provided a guaranteed number of leads for a fixed fee. These prospects typically responded to some offer the third-party media company presented and completed a registration form on the third-party media company's site. On paper, the leads appeared compelling. The cost per name was about 30% that of the pay-per-click program that was running. The data quality was exceptionally high and the titles generally matched the titles the company was targeting. The first sign of a problem occurred, however, when the short-term opportunity creation numbers were investigated. Opportunity creation rates were 25% of the normal opportunity creation rate. When the media company was approached with this statistic, they said these leads needed to be nurtured prior to sending to sales.

Since all leads were nurtured as part of standard operations, the long-term opportunity creation of these prospects was checked. Perhaps the names were high quality and all that was needed was a little nurturing and time over target marketing to generate opportunities.

Unfortunately, looking at the program statistics six months later was not encouraging. Zero opportunities had been created and long-term revenue generation was zero. In this case, encouraging early results for the program actually represented a false positive to an ineffective program.

Ironically, the client continued to do these pay-per-lead type programs since the price was right, and the third-party company could guarantee "leads" for sales, despite the unsatisfactory long-term conversion rates.

Take Action

- Ask the marketing team how they calculate program ROI.
- For leads that were given to the sales team last month, see if it is possible to determine how many have become opportunities.
- Take the long view. Find some old marketing programs in your CRM system that are over two years old and see if any influenced opportunities have closed recently with the campaigns attached.
- Download the metrics tracking sheet from www.storymetrix.com/resources if you haven't done so already and implement the campaign success metrics.

Part IV: People and Processes

Understanding how to measure the opportunity creation process is half the challenge. But once the measurement is in place, how do you impact actual change to the metrics? Implementing the system requires building a measurement system that measures how well the system is actually operating. This is the focus of Chapter 10. Chapters 11 and 12 then look at the organization and key operating meetings and reviews required to implement a metrics-driven marketing organization.

Chapter 10: Housekeeping and Health Reporting

What You Will Learn

- Data quality, business process compliance, and website health measure the health of the revenue-generation factory
- Data quality must be watched so program results are not distorted
- Process compliance is critical to making sure leads are not lost in the database system
- Without a healthy website, valuable traffic is wasted
- Measurement techniques for quality, process compliance, and site health

Overview

Campaign measurement from Chapter 9 is the last piece of the value chain that starts with a prospect and ends with a closed deal. But it is not the last group of measurements required to keep the B2B lead generation system operating. The next set of metrics seeks to measure the actual process of moving prospects through the funnel. These metrics provide insight into whether the process is working correctly. They are broadly broken into measurements around:

- Data quality
- Business process
- Website health

Data quality measures the accuracy and usefulness of data in the system. Over time contacts get old, change jobs, bounce, and unsubscribe. Sales teams also add contacts manually in addition to creating accounts. A database of poor data inflates the marketable size of a company's contact list and can lead to erroneous evaluations of marketing programs and effectiveness.

Business process measures whether agreed-upon processes are being followed. While CRM and marketing automation systems are sophisticated programs, they are designed to support the decision-making and actions of the people who use the system. Unlike an assembly line where raw materials come in one side and finished products go out the other in a straight line, the B2B lead generation process brings in raw materials and assembles a picture of the prospect, but the path through the factory is anything but linear. Prospects move forward, backwards, and sideways, all while new information is being added and old information discarded. Making sure a prospect doesn't get stalled or abandoned during this process takes vigilance.

Website health metrics look at the responsiveness of the website and the availability of content. Poor response time, missing pages, moved pages, or a host of other problems need to be detected early and often in order to prevent prospects from landing on pages that don't exist or take too long to load.

Without these three measurement areas, much of the operating model can quickly become suspect. Sales reps who don't follow up on leads in a timely way will distort program effectiveness. Poor data quality of new leads will cause significant anguish with a sales team that is forced to wade through bad data. Poor website health can destroy the initial response rate on even the best programs. Without the same focus on data health management as lead generation, the effectiveness of lead generation can be cut easily in half.

Data Quality

CRM and marketing automation systems have tremendous daily transactional volume. Data quality is a constant concern, especially with web-based forms and other data upload methods through which prospects enter data directly into the CRM system. Sales rep manipulation of data in the form of creating accounts, opportunities, and contacts can also impact data quality negatively. In addition, data simply gets stale as people change jobs, unsubscribe, add senders to junk mail lists, or simply never respond to an offer. Over time, data quality can quickly decline without vigilant attention from the marketing team.

Contact Data Quality

What's wrong with a database that has poor data quality beyond the obvious impact on sales productivity? First, SaaS (software as a service)-based marketing automation system costs are often based on the size of the database. If 50% or more of the database contains bad data, this could result in significantly higher annual charges compared to those for a clean database. Second, a large database may provide marketers with false confidence about the size of their marketable contacts. Suddenly learning that 50% of your database is made up of bounce-backs or prospects who have not responded to an offer in two years is bound to ruin a marketer's day. Sending emails to people who have never responded also lowers click-through rates for emails and distorts results. Third, sales reps waste time calling contacts that are bad, especially when they are doing cold calling into a lead database. Finally, a database filled with significant amounts of bad data calls into question the quality of all the data in the system. Monitoring data quality is important.

To measure data quality, first define what would constitute bad contact data. If a definition of bad data can be created, then determining the percentage of the database with bad contact data can be easily accomplished. But like many other aspects of B2B marketing, there is not always an easy answer to what is considered bad data.

On one extreme, a contact with no accurate company, last name, email, or phone number is probably not something of value. However, even in this situation, there are gray areas. Many prospects will provide bogus contact information upon first encountering a website form. Over time, as a prospect's relationship with the company improves, it is possible they will gradually increase the amount of accurate information they provide. What initially appears as bad data could evolve into clean data over time.

In addition, many marketing automation systems track prospects on their first contacts with the site via cookies. Regardless of what contact information is provided by a prospect, their cookie uniquely identifies them in the system. Each subsequent visit to the site adds to the web history data. Should the contact ever provide additional details, the past web history detail would provide a valuable record of the prospect's prior anonymous behavior. While a "Mickey Mouse" or an "Acme Corp" contact should certainly be hidden from the sales team, whether this is bad data worthy of deletion may depend on how long it has sat in the database rather than the completeness of the record.

In other cases, prospects may provide accurate name information and email, but inaccurate company and phone number information. Since most marketing automation systems resolve IP addresses for visitors, many times the company information and phone number could be deduced from the IP address and potentially even the email. Whether this type of information is bad data or not is debatable.

Another gray area involves inactive prospects whose data may or may not be bad. If a prospect hasn't responded to anything in over two years, and no one has attempted to contact them for a variety of reasons, are they bad data or just a very inactive prospect? If there are no bounced emails, or attempted contacts to a bad phone number, it can be very difficult to determine if the prospect has bad data.

A possible approach to determining data quality and locating contacts that either contain bad data or are no longer marketable involves implementing a scoring system for quality. Scores would be assigned to a contact based on:

- The length of time they are inactive across the website or in responding in any way to sales rep contact
- Emails that bounce back
- Unsubscribe requests
- Missing phone, email, or name
- Bogus contact information
- Sales reps manually marking a lead as bad data

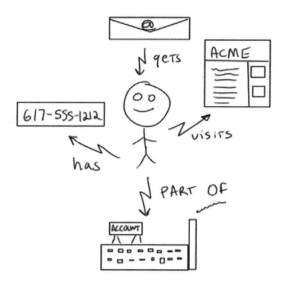

Figure 31: Quality scores are driven by prospects that can get email, visit your site, have valid contact information, and are part of known accounts. The data quality score, however, is cumulative. The failure of a single item to work shouldn't put a prospect in the bad data bin.

Contacts that reach the threshold can be removed from the marketing mix as long as privacy and other aspects of data retention laws are followed. By implementing logic that says contacts marked as "bad data" are only archived after six months of bad data status, you further protect against removing possibly active contacts. If the sales team is able to see which contacts are marked as bad data in their contact screens prior to removal, they can also notify marketing when the algorithm is sweeping up good contacts, or take steps to clean their records to prevent inappropriate archiving.

Once contacts can be labeled as bad data, then counting the number of contacts in the database that scored in this manner represents the easiest way to track data quality. Marketable database size is the actual metric that matters, so taking total database size and subtracting out bad data contacts should yield this number. Marketable database size should not change dramatically each week if bad data scoring routines are run weekly.

Account Data Quality

Beyond looking at the contact level in the database, there are also measures of database quality at the account level. Ideally, a database is being created by marketing and sales of all the potential prospects in the world for your product. This database would be organized by account, with contact names attached to each account.

The concept of an account, however, is a tricky construct. For the marketing organization, an account is a less important data structure. But for the sales team, the account is the vessel that holds contacts and, ultimately, opportunities. In B2B marketing, it is generally the account that is used as the unit of customer interaction and hence the identification of whether an entity has a customer relationship with the company or is simply a prospect. Acme Corp, for example, may be the customer with a bunch of contacts associated with the Acme Corp account. So while John Smith at Acme Corp may be the actual person at the account who is the customer, the entity of Acme Corp is treated as the true customer since the contract is between two companies. If John Smith leaves Acme, for example, Acme is still a customer, but another contact needs to be identified.

Account creation and management is important as a means for sales to communicate back to marketing on the status of a group of contacts. For example, if Acme Corp is a mid-sized company with a single location and single department that would buy a company's product, and Acme becomes a customer, then marketing can use this data designation to send all contacts associated with Acme only customer communication. Sales could be empowered to mark Acme as a customer, or finance could make this designation based on the receipt of a valid purchase order.

Creating and maintaining valid customer lists can be challenging, but directing marketing communications to customers instead of prospects is important. To develop a valid customer list requires that those who are empowered to designate an account a customer mark each appropriate account with this status.

Customer designation of a mid-sized account with a single user represents the easiest case. Problems often arise with account creation and tracking that involves larger organizations or organizations with multiple buyer groups in the same account. Are divisions of a company considered unique accounts? What about different locations within the same division? These decisions impact not only how the account receives marketing information, but also the potential visibility of data to members of a dispersed sales team. Depending on data sharing rules, the same account marked with different sales owners due to different geographic locations could be invisible to two geographically dispersed sales reps, effectively enabling them to work the sames sales opportunity without knowing it.

Account creation is a tricky sales operations subject. Some organizations have solved the problem by making account creation a controlled process. Others allow everyone to create accounts and then clean up or ignore the mess. Either way, measuring the number of accounts with duplicate names is important as a measure of data quality. Standards should be developed on what is considered a clean account and what is considered suspect account information. Potential items for suspect account names could be:

- Duplicate account names (low threshold)
- Duplicate account names with the same address
- Duplicate account names without address
- Duplicate account names without division
- Duplicate account names with the same sales rep

Depending on your sales business processes, a fairly narrow set of criteria could be used to detect duplicate account names. Such criteria might include "All accounts with the same name and same sales rep name but without a corporate division designation". Or, more broadly, "All account names that are the same without different division names" could be considered duplicate.

Business Process Measurements

Moving prospects through the pipeline from lead to opportunity involves sales reps and marketers taking actions, updating lead records, building a holistic picture of an account, developing the opportunity drivers, and developing a picture of the various contacts and actors associated with a deal. In addition, each opportunity has characteristics associated with it, including close date, opportunity stage, and perhaps associated product information. All this information is usually manually entered and changed by sales reps and marketers. This unavoidable manual process introduces the possibility of errors. In addition, since items such as forecast close date and opportunity close percentage represent judgment calls by sales reps, measuring the quality of these judgment calls assists with proper forecasting.

Business process measurements can therefore generally track:

- Instances where there is a clear miss in the required business process
- Instances where the business process appears to be out of an acceptable track

Examples of a complete business process miss include leads not contacted within an agreed-upon time frame, leads that are still being worked by the sales team without a disposition past the service level date, opportunities that are created without associated contacts, or any other measure of business process work that is not correctly entered into the system. These business process misses tend to be fairly black and white. If a rep is given a lead, there is little reason for him to not attempt follow-up within the assigned time frame. If another rep still hasn't closed out a lead many months after he has been given it, something is not right.

Overdue lead follow-up is one of the most important metrics to track. Overdue lead follow-up not only measures if the sales reps are following the correct sales process but also helps ensure leads are routed correctly. If leads are routed to open territories or not routed at all, the sales reps can't follow up on the leads since they are lost in the database. Overdue lead follow-up is a key statistic to ensuring that leads have been delivered to the right people.

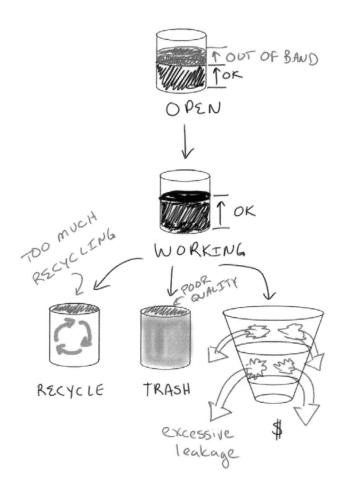

Figure 32: Operating process problems can be detected when there are too many open leads, too high a percentage are being recycled or thrown in the trash, or the opportunity funnel has excessive leakage. These are but a few examples.

Making sure leads have been closed out within the prescribed time frame is important for the marketing team to be able to assess program effectiveness. After sales teams have completed first contact attempts through open leads, those leads containing bad data or prospects that are advanced in the sales cycle are quickly and easily identified when reps either can't make contact or hear back immediately from prospects eager to learn more. The vast majority of leads, however, will not receive a response on the first pass. It is these leads that will generally impact the success or failure of a program due to their greater number. Without a predefined time frame for closing out the lead follow-up phase and working through these leads, it is difficult to get an accurate assessment of a program. Closing out a program before these leads are processed can actually distort final lead disposition reporting. Completing this assessment is important to constantly calibrating marketing spend and also moving the sales team off leads that are not responding and not generating opportunities to other sources of revenue.

Measuring opportunities without associated contacts is another important metric to track in order to ensure marketing programs are appropriately assigned to opportunities. Marketing views programs through the lens of contacts and prospects while sales looks at the world through the lens of opportunities. The only way to link the two is to ensure that when opportunities are created they are mapped to the original prospects that generated them and, hence, to the marketing programs that impacted the original prospects. When sales creates opportunities without any contacts attached to them, it is difficult to map the data from marketing program to contact to the resulting opportunity. Ensuring opportunities have contacts associated with them is therefore important for marketing to be able to attribute marketing program success to long-term sales opportunity creation.

The previous metrics are fairly binary in that they rely on simple queries into the database to determine if a record is within compliance. Harder to differentiate are the business process steps that rely on judgment calls. Many quality issues can be created when such judgment calls are made around opportunities by the sales team. For example, if the average sales cycle is 90 days and a sales rep creates an opportunity with a close date 30 days into the future via a current early-stage sales cycle step, is the rep being overly optimistic or realistic based on what he knows about the opportunity? You can't tell from looking at a single record or opportunity. Only when a skilled sales manager talks to the rep can the likelihood of the opportunity closing be determined. Nonetheless, at least providing visibility to these types of opportunities that appear outside normal operating processes can be a good start.

Another type of clear-cut business process measurement involves the marrying of web analytics data with sales opportunity tracking. For an opportunity to remain viable to close, in general you would expect to see a consistent pattern of web activity from the prospects associated with the opportunity. Failing to see this activity is an indication that either the right prospects are not associated with the opportunity, or the prospects are no longer active on the website. Either case is cause for concern. While the first case could be causing under-representation of marketing effectiveness, the latter case could mean the prospects are no longer interested and the deal is not real. Tracking opportunities that seem to exist without associated website activity within a prescribed time frame can provide a starting point for sales management to investigate the quality of these opportunities.

Many sales opportunities never get to the forecast stage and instead stall at early sales process steps. The longer an opportunity stays open, in general, the less likely it is to close. This is another case in which sales management needs to use pattern recognition and data to determine the optimal sales cycle progress and map this information to the data presented to the sales force. Opportunities that sit for long periods of time at a sales stage are not necessarily bad, but they deserve greater attention from sales management in order to determine whether the deal is still alive.

Skipping steps in the sales process represents another judgment call-type metric that is similar to opportunities sitting too long in a stage. If the sales process requires an ROI but a sales opportunity is forecast to close without a completed ROI analysis recorded, the deal is suspect. Deals can still close without an ROI, and probably do, but this information is important to flag to sales leadership so they can investigate and scrutinize such deals.

The metrics sheet at www.storymetrix.com/reference is just a starting point for business process tracking. The more business processes implemented, the more metrics required. Such metrics should also drive organizations to cautiously implement new processes or only implement processes that can be tracked. Business process metrics are often overlooked and ignored, but are as important as metrics used to track actual sales and marketing effectiveness.

Website Health

Tracking the quality of data in the CRM system can provide an important measure of the health of the revenue generation system. But before data can get into the CRM system, it must be captured by the website. Before the data can be captured by the website, prospects have to find the compelling content they were searching for. A website that is healthy both technically and from a content standpoint is required, therefore, to even get information into the CRM system. Measuring the health of the site, or measuring site errors, is important. Like most types of errors, some are catastrophic and need immediate attention while others are more bothersome and can be slowly improved over time. In general, there are three generic types of health measures for the website: infrastructure health, content health, and page load health.

Infrastructure Health

There are hundreds of reasons why websites may have significant infrastructure issues that make the site go down, be only partially reachable, or simply have too slow a response time. While IT is generally tasked with monitoring the infrastructure, some measure of uptime statistics needs to be incorporated into the CMO's weekly reporting to help ensure an appropriate level of tracking occurs.

If the site is unreachable, such a problem is probably quickly picked up by IT monitoring systems. But what if the site is not rendering 100%? What if form capture pages are not working? What if the video hosting provider is suddenly down, making videos on the site no longer accessible? Prospects are finicky; any point at which the site doesn't function properly reduces lead capture results and should be counted as downtime.

Unless there is a formal reporting mechanism to track cumulative outage time, the CMO may not realize there is any problem with site availability. For that matter, IT also may not recognize some of these problems. For such reasons, the manner in which downtime is reported represents another key statistic. Sites should be considered up when all of the following apply:

- Main site pages and navigation render within x seconds
- All forms are operating
- The site is reachable, not just up
- All third-party providers that impact user experience such as the CRM interface, marketing automation system, video hosting, community functionality, etc. are operational

The Invisible Website

A client site was monitored using one of the SaaS-based services that made sure all the web servers were operating and responding correctly. The site-monitoring software perfectly monitored server health. Unfortunately, it takes more than server health to find a website. DNS servers must correctly point and resolve end user URLs into the specific IP addresses where a company's servers reside. During a switch to a new DNS (domain name system) provider, the DNS transfer was fumbled and the worldwide DNS network was not updated correctly. Prospects looking to find the company would type in the name, only to see that the site was down. The site was actually not down, it just could not be found. Monitored web servers were operating fine as well, so no alerts or alarms were sent. Lesson learned: Site monitoring software needs to both monitor the servers and ensure that site names resolve correctly so prospects can reach the site.

Figure 33: Third-party technology providers to sites such as video hosting services need to be monitored to make sure they are operating. Most IT departments don't monitor these as part of their services, leaving it to marketing to track uptime.

Multiple systems need to be measured to validate uptime, including:

- DNS configuration
- Web serversWeb scripts
- YouTube, Salesforce, and other systems connected to the website

Even with the site up, misconfigurations or a lack of computer resources could impact the site response time for all of its pages. In other words, if the site is placed on underpowered hardware for the amount of expected site traffic and the weight of the content, site response times could suffer dramatically. Long site response times will drive end users away. At some point, if response time exceeds a threshold, the site is considered down although the IT systems may not show it as down. They will simply see highly utilized servers. Understanding this response time threshold is critical to site response tracking.

Crossing the threshold of what is considered poor response time for a customer can be critical. While this is important to recognize, it is actually more important to track how close the site is to approaching this threshold on a weekly basis so the marketing team and IT group can stay ahead of the traffic demand curve and keep a reasonable buffer should the site experience an unexpected increase in traffic. While IT looks at a company's website in terms of utilization statistics of CPU, memory, and network bandwidth, marketing looks at the site through visitors. The total amount of traffic that can be handled with a given hardware configuration is an important capacity metric for both IT and marketing to understand so both sides know how close the site is to full capacity.

Measuring infrastructure health is a multi-step process that must be done. But for the website to deliver prospects, infrastructure health has to be backed up with content health.

$200 More Per Month

A client site suffered an extreme response time slowdown within minutes after winning an award at a major trade show. The announcement caused a surge in traffic that the hardware configuration was not set up to handle. Since the client had not stress tested the site to determine maximum capacity in terms of users, they were not able to handle the order of magnitude increase in traffic. After some quick calls to the internet service provider, more servers were brought online to handle the traffic. Going forward, the CMO requested that IT stress test the site after each major site renovation to determine the maximum number of users the site could handle without a slowdown. Using this statistic, the CMO made sure there was an order of magnitude of reserve traffic capacity on hand in case the scenario repeated itself. Total cost? Only $200 more per month for another order of magnitude of traffic handling, small change since the client was paying about $100 per lead.

Content Errors

A site can be operating correctly, the web servers spinning, the DNS servers pointing everyone to the site, but the content on the site can have errors. Looking at this problem from another angle, IT will typically make sure the site is operating correctly, but the marketing team has to ensure the content of the site contains no errors in its presentation. These errors could include:

- Spelling and grammatical issues
- Confusing sentence structures that make the content impossible to understand
- Broken links
- Missing pages
- Referring site links that refer to missing pages or pages lacking context to the referral
- Pages blocked from search robots
- Pages with poor SEO grades

Spelling errors can be detected with programs that crawl websites. The same goes for grammatical errors. Content that doesn't convey what the author intended is another problem, but there is no system for measuring this except for human A/B testing and reading of content. Broken links and missing pages can be detected and measured. These types of errors are generally referred to as HTTP response codes. The most common are 404 errors that result when site content has been moved. In such cases, a particular URL may no longer exist and a redirect is not in place to move the traffic to a new location. Tracking the number of a site's 404 errors can provide a good measure to help ensure the site has not suffered an unintended content structure change. In cases in which the content on a page does not follow the context from the referring site, such issues can only be detected manually by looking at referring site traffic landing pages.

Figure 34: 404 errors occur when the web server can't find a requested page. Incorrect links or links to pages that no longer exist can cause this.

The final two items on the list of possible website presentation errors involve search engine content. In order for search crawlers to find a website, they need access to the site. Once on a site, the search engine gathers information about what is important from the content and structure of each page. If the page structure is not optimized for the search engine, the search engine may misinterpret or even ignore a page and fail to index it properly.

SEO applications such as Moz.com provide grading to alert site operators to pages that are less than ideal from a content structure standpoint. Defects could include pages that are actually blocked from crawling or pages with poor SEO grades due to their structure. Tracking the number of pages with poor SEO grades, robot blocks, and SEO warnings is important as you strive to ensure your site is healthy from a content standpoint.

Blocking the Robots is Only Good in the Movies

SEO traffic on a client site dropped 30% over a two-week period. The SEO team was stumped as to the cause. The weekly metrics meeting the prior week had been missed due to a scheduling conflict. At the current week's metrics meeting, SEO traffic was once again down. When it came time to look at blocked pages, the blocked pages count had gone up two orders of magnitude. The connection was made immediately that a change to site structure had blocked the blog and a recent Google robot crawl had not crawled the blog, reducing all traffic. The blog had been placed in the "no crawl" category to troubleshoot another SEO issue. The webmaster had forgotten about the change and it wasn't until the team was together again that the story was pieced together and SEO traffic was restored. Lesson learned: Never skip a weekly metrics meeting. The systems are too complex to not understand what is happening each week.

Page Load Times

A site that is operating correctly from an IT perspective, with all the content in the right place, can still have major issues that impact lead generation if the time it takes to load pages is too long. Response times of all pages on a site are governed by multiple factors including the internet connection speed, the size of the web servers, and the back-end databases powering the site. If all pages on the site are the same, one would expect all the pages to have similar page load times. Such a result would essentially reflect the site response time metric reviewed previously under infrastructure health.

But all pages are not the same on a website. Each web page has unique characteristics across several dimensions that impact the page load time to an end user. These characteristics include:

- Number of images
- Sizes of images
- Embedded forms to other applications
- Response time to form submissions from third-party applications
- Java script coding
- Embedded video

- Third-party tracking scripts that run elements such as site response time monitoring, web analytics, and marketing automation systems

Improving response times for pages with a high number of images may not be an IT problem, but is more likely a content management issue. IT provides hardware to meet response times for the entire site assuming an average page size. Marketing can destroy page load times with overly heavy pages and other issues related to the page composition and not the underlying IT hardware.

Figure 35: While seemingly not a problem given high bandwidth connections, page load time is still an issue that needs to be tracked as prospect expectations on page load times constantly increase.

Understanding the average page load time is also important from an aggregate standpoint for a site. Given similar week-over-week traffic mixes, one would expect the average page load time for a site to remain generally the same. Recording weekly page load time averages is the starting point for analysis. Once the average page load time is known, analyzing which pages have the max load times can reveal a good starting point for optimizing the site. Most analytics tools or add-ons provide rankings of pages from slowest to fastest load times. Hence, a key part of the weekly metrics is to also record the load time for the slowest loading page. Tracking page load times is especially important for form submissions to marketing automation systems and landing pages for advertising. While a basic HTML page can be optimized with smaller images or more efficient coding, when third-party services such as marketing automation systems or CRM systems interact with the website, a slowdown in these third-party application servers can also slow down a website. The only way to solve these third-party performance issues is to negotiate with the third party to increase capacity. In other words, it doesn't matter how fast your page loads; if your page contains code or forms from a third-party site, a slowdown in the third party's servers will directly impact the load time of your site.

Bothersome Third Parties

A client was using a marketing automation system from a well-known vendor. All form submissions were delivered into the vendor's database. The vendor had been undergoing dramatic growth and, over time, the response time from submitting a form to getting a thank you page increased to well over 15 seconds. Calls into customer service were met with polite answers about shifting around the node that the client was using. Because the client's database was comprised of over 500,000 records, it simply took time to insert a new record into the database. Over time, it took escalations that nearly resulted in a contract cancellation for the marketing automation vendor to put the proper hardware behind the client's implementation and bring the form submission time down to an acceptable level.

Take Action
- Check Google Analytics for your current page load times.
- Ask the sales team how they determine what is good/bad prospect data quality.
- Look in your CRM system and find all the open leads and determine their age.
- Ask the webmaster how many 404 errors your site had last week.

- Download the metrics tracking sheet from http://www.storymetrix.com/resources if you haven't done so already and implement the process health and website health metrics.

Chapter 11: Building a Team Centered Around Measurements

What You Will Learn

- Importance of lining up people with metrics
- How assigning metrics to people will make you think twice about hiring non "quota-carrying" marketers
- Why classic functional marketing organizations are less than optimal for high-velocity B2B selling
- Why online B2B marketing makes the concept of regional marketing less relevant
- Staff for operations, not administration

Overview

Chapters 1-10 provided an outline of how to measure various parts of the sales process from a very analytical standpoint. The reality for each organization is that, in addition to the metrics, people, processes, and philosophies are required to bring numerical analysis to life. This chapter looks at how to build a metrics-oriented team. Later chapters will look at processes and philosophies.

Aligning Team Members to Metrics

The key to not only measuring but also improving B2B marketing effectiveness is to ensure that all members of the marketing team have metrics they must deliver on a weekly or monthly basis. At the highest level, these metrics are:

- Paid traffic
- Organic traffic
- Conversion percentages
- Nurturing results
- Field enablement

Each of these areas can then be subdivided into component parts. Paid traffic, for example, could be divided into pay-per-click programs and pay-per-lead programs. Organic traffic could be divided into:

- Search engine traffic
- Community sites
- Internal community traffic
- Direct traffic
- Referring site traffic

Referring site traffic, for example, could be further subdivided into:

- Press sites
- Twitter
- General news sites
- Blogs

Blogs could be further subdivided into those run by:

- A-,B-, or C-level bloggers
- Bloggers who are sponsored versus bloggers who are not
- Bloggers who are part of media companies versus independent bloggers

The level of subdivision for each of these metrics depends on the structure of the teams. The key is to make sure each person is responsible for delivering a unique portion of the traffic and conversions on a weekly basis. For a small marketing team, all the referring site traffic may be the responsibility of a single person. On a larger team, all the referring site traffic may be the responsibility of one manager who oversees someone who handles search engine optimization, another person who manages referring site traffic, a third who works the internal community, and a fourth who trolls and works third-party sites like Facebook. For very large organizations that deploy multiple product teams, a single marketer may do the same job across multiple teams. An organization structured in this manner effectively takes a very complex problem and divides it up into component parts, with individuals responsible for solving a unique portion of the problem.

In this structure, the marketing leader has individuals reporting in several key roles:

- Organic traffic manager
- Paid programs manager
- Conversion team manager
- Nurture team manager
- Product marketer (peer)

Organic Traffic Manager

The organic traffic manager is responsible for all referring, direct, SEO, and community-driven traffic to the site. This is a key role since this person or team is also responsible for all content strategy and development. Content drives organic traffic. The organic traffic manager doesn't write all the content, but is the keeper of the content production plan. Since organic traffic is also driven by industry influencers, public relations/analyst relations (PR/AR) management may also sit in this team, along with social interaction and community management.

Such a marketing organization in which PR and AR sit deep in the organization and report into a middle-level manager may represent a drastic change for some. But PR and AR are now just one component that drives organic traffic and interest in the company. It is easy to say that PR is strategic and still requires a report into the CMO. But such a traditional structure falsely focuses the CMO's time on a program that, while important, is less important than tracking critical processes and measurements in a high-volume marketing organization.

The organic traffic manager is essentially responsible for driving, harnessing, and converting all the conversations on the web about the company's products into leads for the sales team. It is perhaps the most key role on the marketing team because, in general, you can't spend your way to marketing success. While this team is not running paid programs, however, it does need funding to purchase content and to sponsor and engage with strategic influencers.

Paid Programs Manager

The paid programs manager is responsible for all programs through which marketing dollars are spent to drive traffic or leads. Paid programs could include:

- Pay-per-click and pay-per-impression programs
- Pay-per-lead programs
- Print and traditional advertising
- Trade shows, events, and user conferences

Paid programs represent the traditional focus point for marketing management. But for high-volume marketing lead generation models, paid programs are only one component of the overall strategy. By placing all the paid programs under one manager, and providing this manager with a goal of maximizing leads, you encourage this manager to use portfolio analysis to maximize output. If paid programs were spread across different managers or groups, resource allocation would become more complex.

Conversion Team Manager

If the paid programs and organic traffic team in general push traffic to the website, the conversion team is responsible for creating the structure, format, and brand of the website in order to convert that traffic to sales leads. While individual landing page content and offers are controlled by the program manager, the conversion team leader must create and optimize landing pages, the brand experience, and the overall site experience to drive conversion rates. Driving high-quality traffic to a poorly designed site with amateur branding is not a recipe for success.

With the brand such an important part of site conversion, placing the branding team with the conversion team is a smart move. Not only can the branding team experiment with brand standards to drive higher conversion rates, but they can perfect the graphics that make brands come alive. The branding team as part of the site conversion team also has the ability to experiment with all different types of graphic elements and colors since they have access to high volumes of traffic. The team can move from the experimental world of opinions to the practical world of experimentation. In addition, since they are busy working on a brand that converts well online, they can also leverage this work in other areas such as pay-per-click advertising, physical trade show booths, and other outlets as they tie everything together into a consistent package. But, first and foremost, the team must be focused on creating a user experience in any medium that converts to leads based on actual measurements, not subjective opinions.

Nurture Team Manager

Assuming the paid and organic teams drive traffic to a well-branded and compelling site, ultimately names will come out of the site that will either be passed to sales or require nurturing. The nurture team's goal is to move prospects towards being sales ready. As such, they operate all the email marketing and other outreach programs to such prospects. Since they are heavily inside the database to support this mission, the team also serves as the operations team for the group. The nurture team understands the flow of data from website form capture to opportunity creation with the sales team. The nurture team represents a critical team for an organization, especially those with large database sizes. The nurture team leans on the conversion team for assistance with email templates and images based on what the conversion team knows works. The nurture team also works closely with product marketing to understand target prospects and ways to engage them in a meaningful email dialogue.

The nurture team needs to deliver conversions from the portion of the database not currently being worked by sales. This will require an active program of new content offers, emails, webinars, and other touch points that will keep the company's brand and solutions in front of prospects. The nurture team uses content from the organic team and listens closely to product marketers and the AdWords team to learn about hot topics in the market. These topics can then be used for follow-on nurture offers.

Since the nurture team is intimate with the structure, workflow, and processes of the database that are required for proper segmentation, the nurture team also serves as the marketing operations group with responsibility for:

- CRM data models
- Marketing automation system operations
- Workflows and processes in this system

If the organic team is the left brain of the marketing organization, the nurture team is the right half of the brain that makes sure everything works properly and prospects become sales leads. They are the operators of the assembly line of processes that takes website conversions and turns them into revenue.

Other Key Team Members

The organic, paid, conversion, and nurture managers make up the core of the marketing organization. There are other key players in the marketing organization that may not be part of the team, but are significantly engaged in day-to-day operations. These roles include product marketing and sales operations.

Product Marketing

If all the work done by the preceding teams delivers leads to a sales organization that is not enabled to engage with prospects, all the effort will be wasted when a sales rep has a poor initial engagement with a prospect. The product marketer is charged with ensuring the field is fully enabled with the right messaging, objection handling, competitive information, financial analysis, and product information. The product marketer doesn't work for the marketing lead, but is responsible as the domain level expert for the product. The product marketer knows the customer prospect, knows how to reach the prospect, and knows what the sales team needs to close deals. This same level of knowledge is spread to the rest of the marketing organization so all marketers can write compelling ads, content, and offers that speak to the buyer.

Sales Operations

The sales operations team is an important part of the marketing team. While it does not report directly into the team, it provides an operational link between marketing and sales. Marketing generates leads that are sales ready. Understanding what happens to those leads as they pass into sales is important to:

- Understand sales opportunity creation rates from a program
- Track leads that are stuck or untouched by sales
- Find leads misrouted or sent to territories without coverage
- Detect sudden increases or decreases in opportunity generation
- Validate that leads generated by marketing are showing up in the sales queue

Hiring and Staffing Roles that Don't Carry Numbers

Not all marketing functions can be measured for their contributions to lead generation. But these groups should be the minority of the organization. They also represent potential candidates for using outside agencies. A marketing organization that has to choose between hiring people for direct traffic/lead-generation jobs versus non-lead number-carrying jobs, will almost always hire first for number-carrying roles.

No CMO gets in trouble for not having enough copy editors, but they will if there are not enough leads. If there is a choice between hiring a copy editor to make ads perfect, or someone to drive traffic from LinkedIn that converts at 10%, the marketer for LinkedIn will get hired every time. But this type of trade-off only works when marketers are assigned numbers. Sales managers must go through a similar process when deciding whether to hire another quota-carrying sales rep or a sales administrator to help with order processing. Both roles are important, but quota coverage, like website traffic coverage, is almost always more important than administration. Non-quota carrying roles, such as a copy editor, should only be added if they can prove they can help marketers with numbers more effectively than one more marketer who delivers a number.

Skill Sets

If most of the marketing functions can be measured by numbers, then analysis and numbers are clearly a key part of the skill set needed by marketers. Given the scope of discussions around metrics and measurement, analytical capability is one of the most critical skills that should be considered when hiring new marketers. Of course a good marketer also has to be good at marketing as well as math. This makes hiring extra difficult. For example, hiring a social marketer requires someone who gets social and can communicate effectively in 140 characters or less, is constantly looking at new social distribution channels, understands your products, but can also do a quick analysis using Google Analytics or HootSuite to understand traffic patterns and other social metrics required to make decisions on future social investments. Going deeper with this analysis, if your social marketer is not analytical and can't crunch numbers to figure out future investments in social and determine what is really working, who can? The social marketer will know the space better than anyone and hence must be responsible for their own analysis. Without this background, when social marketer asks for more resources or a change in strategy, the inability to express why this is important with a careful numerical analysis will fall on deaf ears within a numerically driven team. Social marketing is just one of the examples of a position that requires some analytical insight. Of course nearly every team member needs solid number-crunching skills that include familiarity with Excel.

Team Span

In a small company, a single marketing team is likely to focus on promoting a few products to individual buyers. Larger companies tend to span tens if not hundreds of products and appeal to many different buyers in multiple organizations. What span should a team have with the organization outlined above?

One approach would be to create functional, vertical teams. This is perhaps the most common structure seen in marketing organizations today. Everyone in PR, for example, works for the director of PR, who works for the CMO. While the people on the PR team may handle all the company's products, their reporting structure goes through the director of PR.

This classic functional organization structure is broken for an online marketing-oriented company. The vertical orientation aligns incentives to the functional area and not to individual product results. When marketing could not be measured in terms of traffic and conversions, this alignment made sense. But with a marketing model that is so numbers driven, each team member has to be assigned and charged with delivering their respective numbers in order for the model to succeed. Vertical, functional alignment could be deployed in this manner, but more than likely functional orientation would create a separate incentive and goal structure not aligned to the product team's traffic and conversion goals.

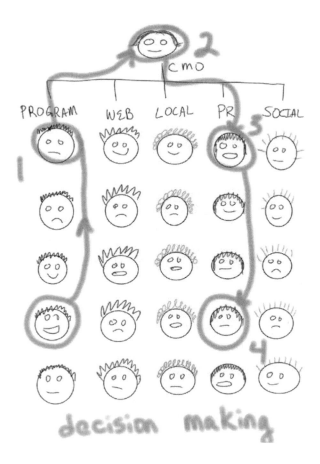

Figure 36: Classic marketing functional organizations introduce too many steps required to run high-velocity lead generation models. In addition, the complexity of operations requires a more integrated team approach.

Compared to a smaller company where the entire marketing team is focused on a few products, a singular buyer, and one sales leader, a larger company with functional leadership is led by managers no longer accountable to a single sales leader, but rather to their own marketing manager. This breaks down the required fanatical (yes, fanatical) focus on daily and weekly numbers.

The key, therefore, is to build out integrated marketing teams, each of which is led by a single marketer with all the key functional roles reporting to him focused on a single buyer, and a single sales leader responsible for the number to that buyer. For example, a company marketing a line of health insurance products with buyers ranging from individuals up through Fortune 500 benefits departments would have a marketing team organized around the different buyers. This makes sense as the team targeting the consumer would vary greatly from the team trying to reach the Fortune 500 VP of human resources. When all of these marketing teams are given all the key components of organic, paid, nurture, and conversion, they can operate in an independent and nimble fashion. All of the marketing leaders for these teams would report into the CMO as the responsible parties for results for their areas.

These marketing leaders of integrated teams would likely be generalists who started initially in a functional role on a team, then rotated through the various positions on the team to get experience in all aspects of traffic driving and conversion. Such experience would then be leveraged when they run the entire team. By creating integrated teams in this manner, an organization also creates an environment in which team members learn others' jobs, providing the ability for team members to change jobs for career learning, and also building camaraderie as the team members learn what works and what does not.

The downside to this structure, however, is that upward mobility is more restricted. There are fewer marketing leads. The organizational structure resembles those utilized by investment banks and top consulting firms where teams of smart generalists work in an integrated fashion to solve problems. This represents a very different type of organization than the highly specialized marketing organizations many companies build.

Smart generalists who can shift roles experience extensive career learning and variety in their jobs. But they may lack deep specialization. In the vertically-oriented functional organization, the head of search engine optimization, for example, may have ten or more years of experience in SEO. Team members may have as much experience. In the horizontal approach of an integrated team, no one member is likely to have that many years in one specific functional area, but may have as many years of experience spread across different roles. To compensate for this, a center of excellence approach is required through which a central team works either part-time or full-time as specialists for all the marketers performing the same function across all the groups. The center's job is to train, spread best practices, and generally nurture the organization's understanding of functional areas. The center of excellence can represent a part-time job for one of the operational team members or a full-time job if the company is large enough, or an outside consultant can be deployed to provide continuous training, technology updates, and an industry-wide view of new developments.

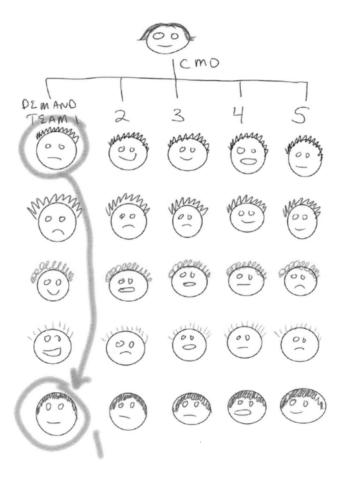

Figure 37: Integrated marketing teams streamline decision-making and align all the experts up with a common goal for demand generation.

Cross-Functional Teams on a Submarine

A 1980s vintage nuclear submarine took around 120 people to crew. The boat's organizational structure was roughly made up of a collection of divisions, with each division a homogenous group of enlisted sailors trained in a particular trade or skill. On the boat, for example, there was an electrical division of 10 or so electricians who knew how to operate, repair, and maintain the ship's electrical system. Another division was comprised of reactor operators who knew the physics and operations of the reactor. Other divisions included sonar operators, radiomen, quartermasters, supply, torpedo men, auxiliary men, and chemists, among others.

These divisions, similar to the divisions in a larger marketing organization, were administrative in nature. A larger marketing team will have multiple divisions, or at least people assigned to specific "trades" such as copy editing, design, search engine optimization, pay-per-click advertising, marketing communications, email marketing, etc.

The submarine was organized into watch sections led by an officer and staffed with a member of every trade who performed specific operational tasks. Sonar was manned by a sonarman. The ship's reactor was operated by a reactor operator with an electrician working the electrical plant. All in all, it took about 20 people from all the different administrative divisions to work together to make the boat move through the water from point A to point B.

During the course of a watch, which was generally six hours, everyone worked for the watch officer, who was the operational head. When not on a watch, a sailor slept, trained, or did work for his administrative group.

The chain of command that was in place while a sailor worked for a watch officer is critical to understand. If the watch officer commanded "Ahead 1/3," the reactor operator adjusted the reactor to make this happen. He didn't first consult his administrative manager to see if it was OK. During watch, he worked for the watch officer.

This is not the case in today's functionally organized marketing teams. The allegiance and alignment is to one's administrative organization and, in many cases, there is no operational management chain, despite there being a near 24x7 marketing operation.

Marketing teams today need to be organized around a strong operational focus and a week-functional administrative organization. This is the opposite of how most teams operate. You don't need 24-hour watch coverage like we did on the boat, but you do need a marketing organization that is lined up to operate effectively.

Global Support

The integrated marketing team structure discussed previously is designed to build a single integrated marketing team to drive product sales focused on a particular buyer. The dimension of geographic scale needs to be considered when constructing a team in this manner. The common approach to geographic marketing coverage is to build teams around countries or regions that duplicate the functions of the central marketing team, or at least localize the programs and processes. This approach is flawed, however, for marketing teams that are heavily online oriented. At the same time, attempting to grow and effectively market globally from one location is not realistic and will impact revenue. The key is to smartly expand the team based on the need to drive operational results as opposed to the need to simply have a local presence.

Flaws in the Traditional Model of Global Expansion

Flaws in the traditional global marketing approach include:

- Creating a local shadow team creates another administrative organization that impedes an integrated operating model
- Much online marketing can be executed globally without having a local presence

- Building remote global teams misses the opportunity to create a globally-oriented marketing team

Second Administrative Layer

Many sales organizations that are built geographically demand their own local marketing since centralized marketing "doesn't understand" the local market. While this can be true, building a second localized marketing team can create significant inefficiencies that end up making local teams less effective than a centralized global operation. A local team with separate reporting structures creates another administrative layer and silo that may compete with the centralized operational team. There may be reasons to do this, but the global reach of online marketing needs to be balanced against the organizational cost of creating a separate administrative silo. Which leads to the second point….

Ads in Mumbai Can Be Managed from Boston (Most of the Time)

Distance doesn't matter for global marketing teams that do a majority of their work online. It is just as easy to run an online ad campaign in Mumbai from an office in Boston as it is to do the campaign from an office in Mumbai, and vice versa. Even in cases in which language differences require translations of ads, white papers, and other materials, native language speakers can be sourced from almost anywhere for the work. Website traffic also doesn't pay attention to internal marketing organizations. Put up a website, and global traffic will pour in regardless of where the marketing team is located. Websites provide the ability to have a global 24x7 trade show without ever leaving your home country. Hence, marketing doesn't need to be in country to accomplish much of what needs to get done.

Missed Opportunities to Create a Globally Thinking Organization

Worse, by creating country-based shadow marketing teams, a company removes the requirement from the centralized team to think globally. Suddenly the country teams are responsible for thinking about their own markets and the uniqueness of some customers around the world. The centralized marketing team then starts down a path of creating offers, content, and other material that is not suitable for other markets.

The centralized marketing team should be thinking globally. It is tough to drive internet traffic to country-specific sites with country-specific offerings. In fact, many prospects will seek out the .com extension for a company since they believe, either anecdotally or through consistent observation, that the .com domain always contains more information than the localized country domain for a company. If the main .com domain only appeals to buyers from a particular region, the marketing team risks losing prospects from other regions. Centralized marketing must think globally since their traffic and marketing reach is global. Local shadow organizations give the central team the excuse that other countries and regions are another team's responsibility.

Central Teams Don't Need to Be Centralized

Despite the use of the word "central", the reality is that a centralized marketing organization does not have to be centralized from a location perspective. There have been endless discussions about the pros and cons of operating physically distributed versus physically centralized teams. But even a CMO who is dedicated to building a physically centralized marketing team can take advantage of remote worker technology to place a member of his team somewhere else in order to provide a more global footprint to marketing. For example, nothing would prevent a marketing team headquartered in Tulsa to have a few far-flung employees. Hire someone to run Google AdWords from Sweden? Why not? Hire a content marketer in the Philippines? Why not? Building a strong global organization can be accomplished with a physically centralized team combined with some smart global hires who can bring global perspective to a team. This approach builds significant team capabilities while not pushing the challenge of global marketing off to another team.

Some Ideas on Staffing Locally

There are exceptions to a centralized approach to marketing, and it is these exceptions that drive requirements for marketing teams to have some manner of local presence. In all cases, however, the local presence should report up to the integrated marketing team and not to a local country marketing manager. Here are some reasons why hiring local marketing may make sense:

- Significant language, time zone, and market differences that warrant modified approaches to going to market based on opportunity size
- Too large an opportunity to ignore
- Difficulty in finding local language experts remotely
- Local trade show and events support

The last two items are fairly self-explanatory, although with the ease of international shipments of trade show containers of all sizes, local show support is less of a concern. The first two items, however, require some discussion.

Dramatically Different Market and Language

"It is different here" is the common expression heard from local marketing or sales teams when describing why marketing programs or sales success in their area isn't up to the same level as other regions. The fact is that it is different everywhere. Even with a country like the U.S., which appears homogenous as a market, there are regional differences between buyers in, for example, Boston and Atlanta. Just looking at these two regions from a B2B standpoint, one can see they have a very different makeup of industries and hence target prospects depending on the products a company is selling. This isn't to understate differences between the Indian market and Germany, but even within India there are huge regional differences among all 28 states. So while it is different everywhere, and some differences are greater than others, the key is to see if these differences really impact marketing and require local marketing assistance.

If the primary go to market channel is online and a particular region is not online and relies on local vendors for advice and recommendations, then courting, managing, and supporting local vendors becomes critical to the strategy. Even in this case, however, it may be possible to market to this region remotely. With a short list of discrete local vendors, assuming language is not a barrier, a marketer can make progress.

In some cases, however, the market may be so large, the language so different, and even the online presence and processes so unlike the core market that there is no way to go to market without someone in country. China, of course, is the best example of this. Different languages, different internet rules and processes, and a massive market opportunity make China impossible to ignore as a candidate for local support. But on the other end of the spectrum, is Australia all that different from other western countries that someone needs to be in country?

Big Opportunities You Can't Ignore

Some markets may be pretty close to the home country in terms of language, culture, and go to market strategy. In some cases, buyers in Australia may be similar enough to buyers in the U.S. that marketing could be run centrally, assuming you have a globally oriented team. But even in these cases, there may be rationale to hire a local marketing team or person. Let's face it, if you hire someone for a specific goal, they will focus on the goal and cause change in the organization to support that goal. Germany is a huge market for information technology sales. Most German IT managers read and speak English. You could make a case that states marketing to Germany could be centrally run from another country, especially since nearly all the marketing is online. Yet the German IT market is too large to ignore its subtleties. Such subtleties extend beyond just local language to include local IT bloggers, local trade shows, local press, and local user groups that would be tough to penetrate remotely. In addition, a global team will not put the focus on driving traffic from a specific country the way a local resource would. Hiring someone in market guarantees a focus on the region. The key is to make sure that focus provides additive results and not just a replacement or local implementation of what could have been accomplished globally.

Trade-Off Analysis to Local Hires

So how do you know when you should hire locally? The advantage of running a metrics-focused IT organization is that each time there is an opportunity for hiring, because the numerical output of each role is somewhat known, CMOs can do a more informed trade-off analysis on which position will add the most incremental traffic and conversions to the marketing funnel.

Let's assume a CMO is given incremental headcount. Should the headcount go to hiring a German marketer or someone on the centralized inbound marketing team to specifically monitor, post, and update on LinkedIn and Facebook? To answer this question, the CMO needs to understand how much more traffic and conversions can be achieved in either case. If coverage of the social media sites will drive 10,000 more visitors per month, and it is not clear how a local marketer in Germany could increase already strong German traffic, then hire the social marketer. If, on the other hand, Germany is completely absent from all site traffic to a company that should be driving significant revenue from Germany, perhaps more focus on Germany is warranted.

Starting with traffic analysis puts the decision-making process on a metrics-oriented footing. This will then enable the more strategic discussion that perhaps, regardless of traffic, the company wants a bigger presence in Germany in order to, for example, court strategic partners. In many cases, this type of analysis will show that centralized roles will generate more global traffic than in country placements. But at some point, the centralized team will hit a point of diminishing returns at which in country marketing is required.

Key Functions for Local Teams

Hiring a local team in market provides the ability for the centralized team to boost their targeting of local prospects. But what functions should a local team take on? In some organizations, local teams, even if a team of one, attempt to take on all functions of the central team since they are the in country team. But this approach does not expand the capabilities of the central team, it just duplicates functions. The real question should ask what functions can and should be done locally that are additive to the global effort? Simply running the Google AdWords campaign locally may not change much in terms of results. The same goes for email marketing campaigns. The key with a local team is to determine which tasks are fully incremental to centralized marketing and optimal when run locally.

If the central team has overlooked key local influencers who only communicate in the local language, then the local team can reach out to them. In fact, the local team is probably the only team that can reach out to them. If the local team notices that the ad, white paper, and email translations are not quite up to standards, they can work with the central team to source another translation agency. If the local team sees that partners are a critical component for success in the country, they should start a partner marketing program. But simply moving global programs to local teams for control purposes causes inefficiencies without adding incremental revenue to the company.

The Dutch Blogger Mafia

At a startup where I worked, the key influencers for the industry were mostly Dutch. It was the oddest coincidence, but this collection of Dutch bloggers had a very large influence over the industry. All their blogs were in English and, because of this, they had a wide reach. A traditional marketing organization headquartered in North America with a European marketing arm planned to assign coverage and relationship building with these bloggers to someone at the European headquarters. In this case, that would have been exactly the wrong move. These bloggers were highly technical and wanted access to both the senior leadership of the company and to the product managers who built the products. All these people were located in the company's North American headquarters. Centrally managing these bloggers worked just fine and gave them easy access to the right people. Of course there is no reason why an EMEA (Europe, Middle East, and Africa) team couldn't manage a relationship such as this. There is just no requirement based on geography that states they must.

Take Action

Establishing an optimal organizational structure is key to implementing a metrics-driven marketing organization. The team structure advocated here is atypical to most marketing organizations, but very typical to organizations that are primarily operational in nature. High-velocity, online, B2B marketing teams are more operational than administrative. Putting in place an operational structure to support a high-tempo marketing cadence is critical to success.

- Map out your customer acquisition flow from traffic source to closed opportunity.
- Align the various teams in the organization against this flow. Are all the steps covered?
- Map out the various metrics for the flow. Are they assigned to everyone?
- Develop a chart of which teams support other teams as "customers". Are all teams aligned? Do teams understand their customers?

Chapter 12: Operating Processes for Real-Time Marketing

What You Will Learn

- How to translate measurement into action
- The four core operating processes
- Why building a marketing operations center is important
- Shocks and changes to the system

Overview

Driving B2B marketing effectiveness requires repeatable process measurement. Only by systematically reviewing, analyzing, and acting on the metrics coming out of the opportunity generation pipeline can the marketing team properly make decisions around resource allocations, have confidence that all systems are operating correctly, and react in real time to market developments and changes. A marketing organization tied to a weekly cadence of results transitions from a static, reactive team that plans 6-12 months in advance for new programs to a high-velocity, real-time operation that is nimble enough to react to competitive moves within hours and establishes the company's relevance as a player in the industry dialogue. A marketing organization that operates in real time knows they have to plan for major product launches and physical events, but also knows that next week their schedule could change if a competitor moves or if this week's marketing program overachieves or underachieves their expectations.

Developing a weekly operation cadence is therefore important. If done correctly, a marketing team can efficiently discuss and act upon a high volume of metrics with just a couple of core interlock meetings each week.

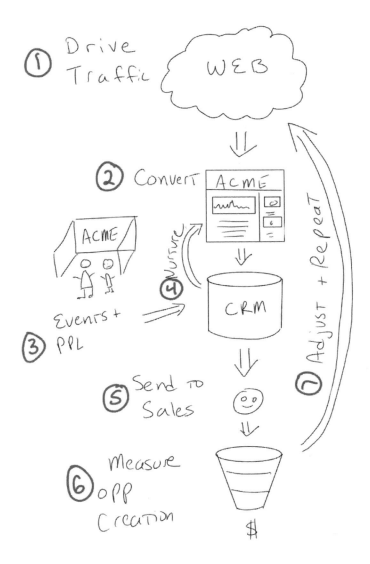

Figure 38: A simple process: Drive traffic, convert traffic, develop offline leads, put leads into the CRM system, nurture leads, send leads to sales, create opportunities, measure opportunities, adjust processes, repeat.

There are four core processes a real-time marketing operation utilizes:

- Real-time metrics measurement

- Historical reporting
- Operational planning or calendaring
- Product launches

Real-Time Metrics Measurement

B2B marketing is a real-time operation. A company's website serves as the 24x7 trade show booth with hundreds, thousands, even tens of thousands of visitors streaming through the booth each day. Beyond the website, social media serves as a listening post to the chatter of the industry, while Google News Alerts or other search programs constantly search the web for new stories and information.

All this chatter is also generally connected. An email campaign that launches a new free product or white paper, for example, should drive website traffic as people click on the email, perhaps a tweet from someone saying "this is cool from this company", and maybe even a post on a site like Reddit. A product announcement from a competitor may trigger a Google News Alert, but could also trigger a blogger to write up a comparison and mention your company, driving traffic to your site and providing an opportunity to reach out and expand the conversation with the blogger in real time. Traffic coming from this blogger's site could be set up to land on a page that specifically compares the products mentioned, making the reference that much more relevant.

Real-time monitoring also helps provide validation that marketing programs are having their desired effect. On a given day of the week, paid traffic to the site from a program like Google AdWords should generally be consistent with similar traffic from the same day of the previous week, unless major changes have been made to the budget or program. If by noon it is noticed that the PPC contribution to the site is off by 50%, that is reason to investigate. Looking at traffic on an hourly basis can also yield immediate feedback on the success of an email campaign. Real-time monitoring products like Clicky provide the ability to easily compare real-time traffic by the hour week over week. If a company does their email blasts the same day of the week, at the same time, the campaigns with the better performance will be immediately noticeable by the higher traffic.

Despite this stream of events going on each day, many marketing teams don't watch what is happening in real time. It is like having a trade show booth but not staffing it except once a week, even though the trade show floor is open all day. Since marketing happens in real time, marketing measurement needs to take place in real time. To accomplish this, marketing must first and foremost adopt a real-time posture to marketing metrics measurement. The virtual world must be placed directly in front of the marketing team as a constant reminder that there are "people out there" every minute making purchasing decisions about the company.

Making the Virtual Present with a Marketing Operations Center

Marketing organizations doing online B2B marketing need to physically place themselves in an environment that fosters this real-time monitoring and collaboration of what is happening in the virtual world. If you were running a trade show, your trade show booth captain wouldn't be sitting 100 miles away in a cube, checking in on email every few hours. For a major show, the booth captain would be in the booth directing operations, talking to people, and making sure everything is running smoothly. The same is true with the virtual world. Marketing teams need to immerse themselves in the metrics, traffic indicators, Twitter feeds, and email alerts that represent the flow of prospects through their systems. To do this, marketing should physically create a control center-like room called a marketing operations center or MOC, to place the marketing team in the center of the action.

The marketing operations center not only provides invaluable information about what is occurring on the website, but also serves as a constant reminder that there are real people and real prospects on the website all the time and the site is not a virtual abstraction. A MOC should be designed so that all marketers can easily look up from their desks and see on multiple monitors the status of key systems and indicators. Team members can look up, notice trends, process these trends, and sometimes engage in conversation with others about what they see. "Hey look, someone is tweeting about our new product and look at our traffic to the site!" Or: "Bob, did you send out the email yet? I don't see any bump from your weekly email campaign."

Key screens to use in a MOC for marketing measurement are:

- **Real-Time Traffic Statistics** – Current site visitors, traffic from same day a week ago, top landing pages, top referring sites. Google Analytics or specialty vendors such as Clicky can provide this. Real-time statistics will also reveal traffic surges caused by email campaigns or sudden news events that drive traffic.
- **Site Health** – Infrastructure status monitoring and/or response time measurements to ensure the site is performing correctly. While infrastructure monitoring may also be captured in IT, response time measurements may not be monitored by IT unless there is an issue. Real-time monitoring of response statistics provides validation that all the systems are operating correctly.
- **Social Monitoring** – Monitoring the social universe is a task in and of itself. While a social monitoring screen doesn't replace in-depth social monitoring, providing a display of relevant tweets from key influencers and competitors does bring the external conversation into the marketing room in real time. When marketers learn that a competitor, for example, is running a webinar and then watch as everyone online gets excited about it, they will react. TweetDeck is a good tool to have on display for this, as is TwitterFall.
- **Daily Metrics** – Each day, the website has to produce leads for the sales team. If marketing metrics are being driven on a weekly basis, achieving weekly numbers requires daily performance goals. Posting daily numbers also keeps the team focused while providing early warnings to failed programs.

Figure 39: Creating a marketing operations center makes "virtual" traffic come alive and aligns the marketing team with the concept that people are making buying decisions every minute of every day about their products.

The MOC provides the minute-by-minute pulse to the marketing organization that makes it clear there are prospects "out there" constantly stopping by the company. While real-time monitoring is critical, the next step is to look back over a week or more to spot trends and gain additional insight into marketing operations.

Historical Metrics Reporting

Real-time reporting is good for instilling a sense of urgency. But real-time reporting is highly reactive, and designed to be so. Historical reporting is where a marketing team can start to look at some trends, or at least confirm that systems, processes, and programs are working properly.

Historical reporting generally looks over the preceding week, month, or year and records results across all the key metrics. This book contains a significant amount of metrics that could be reported on a weekly or monthly basis. The key is to use the metrics that make sense and record them at a frequency that is relevant to the business. Metrics that are not relevant should be discarded and new metrics added as needed.

Historical reporting not only records what happened during the previous time period, but also serves as a point-in-time snapshot of the status of the marketing effort. Freezing reporting at this snapshot is important as many marketing systems don't record for historical purposes reports at a point in time. Say a database contains 1,000 lead records on March 1. If you run the report a month later on April 1 and the system contains 2,000 lead records, only if the reading taken on March 1 was recorded will you have a reference to understand that the database size has doubled in the preceding 30 days. Historical snapshots of data are critical to effectively assess performance.

Delivering numbers at whatever time interval is deemed correct, whether you are reporting referring site traffic numbers or direct traffic numbers or campaign results, should occur in an organized fashion that is built around a recurring metrics review meeting. The metrics review session provides the foundation for keeping the marketing team focused on whatever cadence the CMO has set.

The metrics review meeting also provides the opportunity for the senior leader to see the entire picture of how everything worked in the preceding period. But its value goes beyond the leadership team. With the entire team looking in detail at the numbers for the previous period, the entire team starts to see how everything fits together to drive results.

In order for such a review to be successful, each metric should be the responsibility of a single person. If the organization is structured as discussed in the previous chapters, there is a natural person responsible for each line of a metrics review. If no one person is responsible for a metric, or it is the responsibility of multiple people, then something is probably wrong unless the metric simply can't be broken into component parts. While total site traffic, for example, is the culmination of inbound marketing, paid programs, email marketing, and direct traffic, each of the component parts can be assigned to a person for accountability. Delivering total traffic is theoretically the CMO's job, but the only way for the CMO to deliver gradually improving total traffic numbers is to break each number down into its component parts and assign those parts to individuals who are then charged with delivering their pieces of the model. These individual components can then be broken down even further to additional individuals depending on team sizes. Inbound organic traffic could have multiple team leaders or multiple teams working on it, from SEO teams to blogging teams to PR teams. PR could be tasked with delivering traffic from press and influencer teams, blogging teams could be tasked with delivering relevant content that drives traffic through organic search to the blogs, and SEO could be tasked with delivering overall SEO traffic. The ability to continue to cut and divide traffic into component parts is critical to establishing effective accountability assignments that start to create a traffic-obsessed culture.

Each person reporting their share of a metric must be able to report the source of the metric, understand what they are measuring, and understand the interaction of their metric with the other parts of the system. It is this interaction which ultimately improves overall marketing efforts. When each team member understands how the system operates and how all the metrics are related, learning on the part of one team member can be applied to others, even if they are responsible for a different marketing channel.

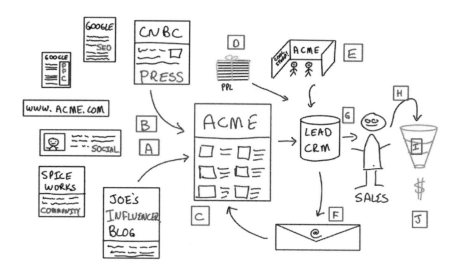

Figure 40: With each part of marketing operations instrumented (A-J), the people responsible for these areas should report on weekly status and progress. Such a system should uncover any abnormal trends but, more importantly, it should provide the team with simple validation that everything is working.

If pay-per-click traffic starts to go up and overall site bounce rate also goes up, the paid traffic owner should be able to connect the dots between overall site bounce rate and potentially lower-quality paid traffic. The increase in bounce rate should be investigated and the cause determined and shared with the team. Another example could involve a particularly successful email campaign. If traffic from an email campaign is higher than normal, the team should be able to understand why that particular email was more successful than past campaigns. Armed with this information, they can then adjust paid programs, the future content production schedule, and even events and webinars. If traffic from a campaign was higher than normal but conversion rates on the site were lower than expected, this information is also important for all to understand, especially since most marketers must use forms at some point for conversions.

Collecting and reporting on key marketing metrics can be accomplished by building sophisticated data warehouses or by simply sharing a common spreadsheet using Excel or an application like Google Docs. Marketing measurement by definition will undergo significant changes as metrics are swapped into or out of executive level reports. This makes the use of spreadsheets an ideal, but less than elegant, solution. In addition, since the accurate picture of marketing spend comes from multiple data sources such as website data, CRM system data, and YouTube metrics, building a data warehouse to house all this information using APIs is certainly a possible but large undertaking. Using shared spreadsheets is one way to get the project started.

The periodic metrics review meeting should last no more than an hour and involve a quick review of each metric in a sequence that makes sense for the team. Roll-up calculations such as traffic by geography or traffic by source should be used when needed to provide the global picture of marketing results while also allowing people to drill down to their component parts.

Weekly Calendar Process

With a weekly, monthly, quarterly, and yearly metrics cadence operating along with daily real-time reviews, the next major element to implement is a closed-loop process that takes this information and feeds it back into the marketing process in order to tune programs for success. If particular white paper programs or online ads are more effective at generating traffic that conversions, such information should be taken by the other teams and incorporated into their programs.

Log Taking

Taking readings on operating machinery is a time-honored tradition in the Navy. Literally in every space on a submarine when I was on board in the 1980s, while underway there was someone with a clipboard walking around at set intervals, taking measurements on the various temperature, pressure, voltage, and flow gauges mounted on all the electrical and mechanical systems in the boat. Every 15 minutes to perhaps an hour, the same readings were recorded. Over the course of a six-hour watch, while steaming at the same speed and depth submerged, which could be typical of a transatlantic crossing, not much changed unless ocean temperatures changed significantly. The result was a somewhat mind-numbing six hours spent looking at the same readings hour after hour.

On the flip side, however, this level of attention to the various readings on the ship made the crew very connected to the heartbeat of the ship's operations. Changes in readings were quickly noted and, if they were not out of specification, were the subject of at least some amount of analysis in an attempt to determine why they had occurred.

For historical review, at least once a watch the logs were taken to the engineering officer for review of longer-term trends. This review process enabled a second supervisory look at the data. While marketing operations don't have to achieve such a level of detail and review, recording and analyzing operating metrics are important in order to gain an understanding of how the marketing system is operating.

The starting point for the closed-loop process is the marketing calendar that spells out how each of the major traffic-driving groups will be operating over the coming weeks or months. The calendar takes into account product launches and new content that is delivered, along with events. With a real-time marketing operation, however, the calendar can be planned out as far as possible, but news from competitors and last-minute changes to a product launch or other event will conspire to disrupt the schedule. With at least a tentative calendar in place, however, it should be possible to make weekly estimates on traffic and conversions for several weeks to months into the future. This forecasting process is important for determining if additional resources are required. For each of the various marketing channels, general estimates can be made of traffic and conversions based on the programs run in the past. With the calendar setting the weekly tempo of operations, regularly scheduled calendar meetings then provide feedback as to the effectiveness of the calendar.

In order for such a calendar meeting to be successful, its rules should be similar to the metrics meeting. Each person responsible for delivering a part of the marketing programs for the coming weeks needs to present what is happening in that area for a given week. This list might include sections dedicated to:

- Product launches
- New white papers and videos
- Blog postings
- New content bundles that create additional white papers, videos, etc.
- Events – physical and virtual
- New paid campaigns kicking off
- Website promotional tiles
- Major site rework
- Sales training and other enablement actions

With weekly planning underway, there is rarely the need to hold semi-annual planning meetings that attempt to plot out marketing operations months in advance. Marketing becomes real time, with real-time pressure to produce new content, programs, and events. This shift reflects the difference between the old-factory systems of the 1970s that used to stock parts that would be pulled off the shelves when needed and the lean manufacturing that started in the 1980s. Lean manufacturing resulted in tremendous improvements in quality, costs, and flexibility. Real-time marketing can, too.

Changes to the System

While feedback from weekly numbers can drive corrections to the marketing calendar, other changes to the system can cause disruptions, as well. Product launches are perhaps the biggest change. New products or products with new features can alter content strategies, keyword listings, community topics, and even top influencer lists. New products or new features can require updates to an entire collection of field readiness checklists and new-hire training materials. Product launches can require a detailed checklist to make sure all elements of marketing are ready to push out new product news and information on all fronts.

Competitive announcements can have similar impacts on marketing operations that end up not only showing up in weekly metrics, but also forcing a change throughout the organization in keywords, content, blog postings, and even influencers.

Other changes that can impact the marketing system include changes to Google search algorithms and social media site operating processes or policies. Updates to Google search algorithms are perhaps the greatest source of continuous change in the industry for online marketers. Companies are constantly attempting to game the algorithm while Google is constantly working to provide the most relevant results. Each time the algorithm changes, it impacts page rankings and site traffic. For companies that use black hat SEO techniques for traffic driving, such algorithm changes can introduce dramatic changes to organic search traffic.

Beyond algorithm changes, operating policies can also impact traffic. LinkedIn, for example, used to send out daily digests in which it was fairly easy to be included. The resulting email blast from LinkedIn to thousands of users resulted in traffic to your site. A change in policy regarding how LinkedIn conducted the blasts and selected blast content made it increasingly difficult to be included. What had been a regular source of traffic from LinkedIn emails went from a high number as a percentage of daily traffic to zero overnight.

While existing social media sites can change policies that have an immediate impact, new social media sites and applications can shift the landscape of traffic in a matter of months. Constantly experimenting with these applications is the best way to determine which sites might assist in lead generation and which sites are not yet ready or are simply ineffective.

While social media sites may introduce new venues for traffic, market changes — especially in emerging markets — can disrupt the weekly and monthly cadence of a marketing team. Depending on the stage of a market, emerging concepts and ideas can require an overhaul of keyword lists, website structure, competitive landscape, etc. These changes could be news driven or the result of gradual market shifts. Some mainstream examples include the rise of hybrid cars for automakers or those who market products to the car industry. If you are an aftermarket supplier of car floor mats, the increase of hybrid cars would require that you start buying keywords or marketing to people looking for "floor mats for hybrid", etc. In technology markets, such changes can occur over the course of months. Larger market leaders can start a discussion about a new technology or concept with unique terminology the industry eventually adopts. New terminology surrounding technological developments could be rich sources of traffic as bloggers write about the concepts, people seek out white papers, and others look for new products that are now available.

Perhaps the biggest change that can impact site operations involves the migration of the site as a result of the company's acquisition. An entire book could be written on how to do this. Suffice to say that this is a very disruptive event. All link and referring site traffic goodwill is potentially disrupted in such instances. All the painstaking form optimization and content work is disrupted. Theoretically, if acquired by a larger company that actually drives more traffic to products, the acquired company will come out ahead. But this may not always be the case. On the flip side, if you are the acquiring company, you suddenly have access to what is hopefully a rich set of traffic and conversions driven by careful SEO and referring site strategies. Leveraging without destroying this traffic can result in buying SEO rankings, favor with key influencers, referring site links, and a high level of direct traffic. The key is to not squander this resource while also providing the acquired site the benefits of the larger company.

Help Lost Traffic Find Its Way Home

A client company had acquired multiple companies. As an experiment, I went hunting for the artifacts of the acquired company's traffic. Landing pages with massive amounts of what appeared to be organic traffic looked suspicious. Why was all this referring site traffic from what appeared to be disparate sources linked to a page deep in the site structure?

Looking at keywords and referring site URLs revealed that this was a redirect from the old site that had been shut down. What was fascinating was the treatment the traffic was given. Before the site was shut down, the traffic had landed on highly contextual pages painstakingly tuned for the traffic arriving on the site. Post acquisition and site shutdown, the traffic was dumped on a generic landing page without any context. If the acquiring company had massive traffic to replace the traffic from the original site, then this would not matter. But the acquiring company had little presence in the market, which had been one of the prime reasons for acquiring the company in the first place. So while the acquiring company got the products and people they desired, they neglected to take into consideration the value of the website traffic. In the name of integration, they shut down the old site, and eventually lost all the traffic from the old company.

Take Action

Building out a steady cadence of calendar sessions and weekly or monthly metrics sessions and driving value from such sessions is not an easy undertaking. Especially for organizations in which accountability to numbers is not part of the marketing culture, getting everyone to stand up each week and report out numbers may take some time. Similarly, it takes time to figure out which developments deserve attention and which can be safely ignored. But with patience, and a time limit for these meetings, marketing teams can develop into metric-oriented operators that drive enhanced business results. Take action:

- Set up a monitor on the marketing floor and put up the real-time traffic analytics for your site. Can your team explain what is happening?
- Implement a weekly calendar meeting that looks at all aspects of marketing for the next 6-8 weeks. Are the plans integrated? Do people feed off other peoples' ideas and plans?

- On Monday afternoon, assemble your marketing team and ask them what happened the week before. How many leads went to sales? Can you find the leads in the CRM system? Does sales know the leads are there? Ask about traffic, conversions. What was hot in the market last week on social media?
- Download the metrics tracker off www.storymetrix.com/resources, send it to your team, and ask them what metrics they want to report on a weekly basis.

Part V: The Soft Factors – Philosophy and Success

With all the focus on numbers and measurement, the final part of this book contains little to no metrics. Chapter 13 presents some philosophy statements on how to operate a metrics-driven organization. Chapter 14 provides some indicators on what success looks like. Certainly numbers going in the right direction represent a sign of success, but there are other, more subtle indicators that the process is working that should not be ignored.

Chapter 13: Philosophy

What You Will Learn

- Eighteen philosophy points that may contradict other parts of this book
- Why SLAs, awareness, and too much measurement can be bad
- Why SLAs, awareness, and too much measurement can be good

Overview

Without the philosophical grounding of a B2B operational strategy, when confronted by closet skeptics with seemingly innocuous and logical statements such as...

- "Our programs are for awareness and can't be measured"
- "Our programs are different"
- "Marketing operations does all the measurements, we don't know how"
- "I can't get access to that system"
- "1% is good"

...it is easy to drift off course and not implement a truly metrics-driven marketing organization. This chapter contains philosophical sections that provide a departure from some of the drier metrics discussions in previous chapters. A few of the ideas are a bit extreme, but hopefully they make the point on a philosophical framework for operations.

The following items represent philosophical statements to guide operations for a real-time marketing organization.

#1: Eliminate What Doesn't Work

Why measure everything? Most marketers strive to figure out exactly "what works" to drive leads and opportunities for the company because they believe this is most important. The opposite, in fact, is true. The goal should be to eliminate what doesn't work even when it gives the appearance of working. Marketers push statistics of open rates and click-through rates among other measures as badges of success. Yet without proof that these results deliver sales opportunities, such metrics are meaningless. The challenge with trying to tie opportunities to deals is that it can take many months for a deal to work its way through the sales process. Marketers need immediate or close-to-immediate feedback regarding whether a program has a high likelihood of success. Waiting six months is probably not a good option.

There is a solution. By approaching programs with a skeptical point of view and looking to eliminate what doesn't work (as opposed to trying to find what does work), less time will be wasted on the majority of programs that don't work. For example, if there is a sudden increase in click-through rates and leads from Google from a country with no discernible market for your product, that should make you suspicious of the possibility that this is high-quality traffic. If you are just looking at the surface metrics of an AdWords campaign, you may not detect this. In fact, this increase in leads could be viewed in a positive manner. More leads, more clicks, it is all good. But if you are taking a holistic approach to your marketing engine, you may notice the traffic spike from this country, which leads to an investigation into the cause and the newfound wealth of pay-per-clicks from this country. If you approach this with the attitude of "Wow, this works! Look, we are getting leads from this country!" you are going down the wrong path. The approach needs to be "Interesting. I wonder if these leads are any good because this behavior doesn't make any sense. There is no market for our products in this country." Finding the programs that don't work and the results that don't make sense should be the goal in order to avoid sending leads to sales that will never convert.

An extreme case of why being skeptical is key can be found in the "guaranteed" lead programs that many old-school media companies run. What can be better than a "guaranteed" lead in terms of volume and cost? Marketers could spend money all day long to get these guaranteed leads. The cost per lead is predictable, the supply is predictable, and the data quality is high. Without taking the skeptical view of this, all appears well. The skeptical marketer, however, tries to discern if any of these leads have value. The skeptical marketer tries to understand how these programs really work. The skeptical marketer tracks the opportunity conversion rate soon after the leads are delivered to sales and talks to reps to get anecdotal feedback on the leads' quality. The skeptical marketer's goal is to assume these are poor-quality leads, and to set out to find the data that will prove them otherwise.

#2: Don't Do Anything without Measuring

If you are considering spending money on a program or spending marketing labor on an organic program, the first question after the idea is proposed should be "How do we measure this?" Often a program that at first doesn't appear to lend itself to measurement can be altered to be measurable. Without this constant focus on "How do we measure this?", marketing can spend oodles of dollars and resources pursuing activities that feel good, but can't be quantified as successful. In the olden days (10 years ago), this was OK. The problem now is that there are so many measurable programs that if you are spending money on something that can't be measured, you are ultimately not spending money or time on something that has a predictable result. Ask your sales team if they want you to spend money or time on program X that delivers Y leads, or program Z that you can't measure, and you can imagine the answer you will get.

In addition, with so many new types of costly and involved online programs available for marketing to consider, setting up clear measurements of success is critical in order to enable the organization to experiment safely with select new programs.

Asking the question "How do we measure this?" can also yield some great program modification ideas. For example, trade show operators are great for offering premium sponsorship packages that allow the hanging of huge banners in entrance hallways. Most companies do this for "awareness" ("Awareness" should be a banned term in marketing organizations, but more on this later). Most of these banners say the company name and "Visit Us in Booth 123". As designed, this is not a measurable program. No one is going to say "Hey, I saw the huge banner you paid $40,000 for in the entrance hallway and decided to come by your booth." While walking by the banner the CMO may be happy and the CEO may be happy, but the sales team shouldn't be. That $40,000 could have been spent on direct demand generation. Unless, of course, you can somehow measure the success of the banner. Why not put an offer on it: "Visit our booth, mention this banner, and get XYZ"? Problem solved. Banner in entranceway = xxx number of visitors to the booth. Are they incremental visitors? Who knows. Are they high-quality visitors? Take notes and measure. Using this methodology, marketing can do a simple analysis:

- Banner cost: $40,000
- Number of visitors who came by referencing banner: 500
- Cost/banner visitor: $80
- Cost/regular trade show visitor: $40
- Quality of banner visitors: High
- Prior-year visits without banner: 2,500
- Current-year visits with banner : 3,200

Would you repeat this banner placement? That is a subjective call. But at least there seems to be some data that shows people read the banner, they are qualified people, and they came by the booth. You also get all the impressions and awareness (using a banned term) for people who many not stop by, but at least saw your banner. The right decision? There is no right or wrong in this case, but at least you have some data points that support the decision.

$10,000 Popcorn Machine

At a recent trade show we attended, a company had paid $10,000 to rent a popcorn machine from the show organizers. To get popcorn, an attendee had to get their badge scanned. The smell went through the entire hall and it was a bit irresistible. It seemed like an interesting idea for our next show. But what about the economics?

To figure out the economics of the popcorn machine, we wandered by and struck up a conversation with the operator towards the end of the show. The operator told us about 1,000 people stopped by the machine during the show for a cost per name of $10, which seemed compelling.

I wanted to see the follow-up from the company who had rented the machine, so I dutifully handed over my badge and, sure enough, two weeks later I got some generic message about the company and the trade show. No reference to the popcorn machine, no reference to how I even knew they were at the show.

The next year I asked our trade show team to get the popcorn machine. I really wanted it. I like popcorn, and thought we could do a better job at executing. At $10 per name, the popcorn machine was an extremely cheap source of raw names. We had no illusions, however, that these people would have recognition of our brand or even of what we did. To help offset this, we decided to staff the machine with our own people so they could strike up conversations.

When our trade show manager went to book the machine, unfortunately, we found the machine was already rented for the North American show, and the European show didn't do popcorn, but rather smoothies. Question #1: Do Europeans drink smoothies at a per trade show attendee rate that matches or is higher than the per trade show attendee rate at which North Americans munch popcorn? Same concept, different food, different food group, different location. We would have to see.

We rented the smoothies station, staffed it with our employees, and starting scanning badges.

What happened with the program? Disaster! Numbers in Europe were half the numbers in the U.S. due to the machine location and, perhaps, European appetite and consumption of smoothies. Worse, even though we followed up with a highly topical email specific to show smoothie consumption that included our most compelling offer, the people scanned at the smoothie bar did not convert into any type of qualified leads. The machine experiment did help us tap into a new source of names of people who did not stop by our booth, but without conversion to a lead, it is tough to justify the expense. The machine was located on the opposite end of the floor from our booth and, surprisingly, there was little overlap with our booth attendee list. But there was no way to justify the expense due to the poor conversion rates to actual leads and opportunities for sales.

The experiment was fun, we had measurable goals, and we could leverage our popcorn learning when making similar decisions about trade show promotional add-ons going forward. Often, when an idea or program was proposed, someone would say "Remember the data from the smoothie machine."

#3: Measure What You Can, Not What You Want

Every CMO or VP of sales wants the perfect answer to whether a particular lead and/or marketing program generated a certain amount of revenue. They want to know the one white paper or banner ad that is the secret to revenue. This pursuit is similar to looking for the fountain of youth. It is the search for the holy grail of measurement. Unfortunately, it is difficult, if not impossible, to make definitive judgments for end-to-end program execution due to the complexity of B2B marketing. A single sales opportunity is created through too many marketing interactions, multiple prospects, and many starts and stops to a deal. There are always exceptions to this. You might get a single banner ad to trigger someone to come through and buy. But without careful post-deal investigation, you might miss that this prospect already knew of the company through a co-worker who visited your trade show booth. There are just too many variables.

The philosophy and direction, therefore, needs to be to measure what you can, not what you want. You can't always measure what you want, but you can combine measurements of things that are possible with some plausible assumptions in order to gain confidence that your program should not be rejected.

For example, if a marketing program is run that has high data quality, a high rate of acceptance by the sales team, and a high rate of opportunity creation, then it is likely this program should not be rejected even if it is impossible to measure whether this specific program caused prospects to ultimately purchase products. Somehow the program appears to be positively correlated with deals closing. Is it the cause of deals closing? You could spend weeks looking at all the players, deconstructing their web visits and the marketing offers they accepted, and analyzing things such as the order in which they accepted the offers and still not come up with a definitive answer as to what caused people to purchase. So many elements of such a complex process are tough and very likely impossible to measure. But you can state with certainty that prospects appeared to have been impacted by this program on their journeys to purchasing your company's products.

#4: Consistency in Measurement

Marketers like to claim things can't be measured since programs are all different. But, in reality, programs are not all that different. Whether you are sending emails, driving web traffic, or operating a trade show booth, in general you are following the same process. You are providing impressions or attracting attendees, hoping for one or multiple conversions from website browsers or booth visitors, watching for form completions, then measuring the conversion of leads to opportunities. Cost per names, cost per leads, cost per opportunities all represent the same metrics down to which programs can be distilled.

There are differences, but they tend to be more between the target of the marketing effort as opposed to the individual tactics used. Comparing the tactics and costs of reaching CEOs to the tactics and costs of reaching IT administrators is not fair or proper. But the programs targeting IT administrators can and should be compared against each other using standard metrics regardless of whether programs were delivered online, offline, or through direct mail. Each of the programs may have its own set of program-unique metrics, but since marketing is an allocation game, all programs must be compared against similar criteria so resource allocations can be made effectively.

#5: Be Very Wary of Awareness

Digital marketing efforts enable the marketing organization to put solutions in front of prospects who are in immediate pain and need a solution. Whether through paid advertising focused on solutions, content marketing that contains answers to common problems, or trade shows that enable face-to-face qualifications, a significant amount of effort can be spent both in time and money on finding prospects with pain. We will call this pain-based marketing. For the sales team, nothing is better than receiving a sales lead of someone who has a pain that their product or solution can solve.

If you accept this assumption, marketing allocation of both dollars and time to broad-based awareness campaigns that don't deliver measurable results or leads would always be second in priority to lead-based programs. In fact, if you could focus 100% of your time and energy on demand generation efforts and leads for sales that filled the sales pipeline and grew the business, you would not have to spend effort on anything called "awareness". Imagine telling your sales VP that you are not going to supply 1,000 leads, but rather an awareness campaign of uncertain results.

So why do organizations spend money on "awareness" and somehow believe they don't have to track results? The answer, I believe, is that when lead flow to sales is less than desired, sales and marketing determine it is due to awareness. This could be the case, but until the efforts to find pain candidates go past the point of diminishing return, the effort spent on awareness is further robbing the team from direct lead generation. More importantly, there is no guarantee that all the awareness spending will result in more leads. Theoretically, awareness spending would result in higher direct traffic, higher click-through rates from existing referral sites, and great click-through rates for all other online advertising. But quantifying the impact of this awareness is extremely difficult, if not impossible.

There is a way to spend on awareness, yet still get results. If you consider that demand generation efforts provide a significant amount of collateral awareness, spending money on impressions that result in direct lead generation also means that all those unclicked impressions certainly create awareness. For every paid ad impression that contains your brand and a call to action, awareness is created. For every piece of content or tweet or posting on LinkedIn, awareness is created. In fact, by specifically targeting end users with content and advertising that is focused on their problems, marketers create significant amounts of awareness. The difference is that the awareness is a by-product of the demand generation focus.

So when would resource investment for "awareness" make sense? In high-volume B2B lead generation efforts, awareness spending seems to make sense when trying to get in front of niche audiences. If potential investors or strategic partners read the trade industry press, getting articles and mentions in this press probably won't drive traffic and leads, but it will open strategic doors for the company. If specific industry bloggers are very influential on judging panels or in the content and reviews they write, spending money on awareness on their blogs probably won't drive direct traffic from the ad spend, but will buy awareness with these judges. Finally, industry analysts many times require subscriptions to their newsletters or content sites for them to engage with you. If purchasing these subscriptions also gets you client access to these analysts to tell your story, this type of influencer awareness is tough to measure but does drive longer-term results.

Awareness spending for the sake of awareness is a difficult proposition when time and resources can be spent on direct lead generation efforts that also provide collateral awareness. However, spending on awareness with a strategic intention in mind remains a worthwhile endeavor. The problem comes when marketers confuse awareness spending with somehow increasing lead generation.

Awareness is for People Who are Afraid of Metrics

At one company where I worked, we tracked referring site traffic from media sites separate from other sites. We hired an outside PR firm, and we wanted to see whether our PR efforts drove any traffic or lead volume. This drove the internal PR team crazy along with the PR agency themselves. "PR is for awareness" was their rallying cry every time they put up "reach" statistics or data showing huge numbers of story placements. "But you didn't drive any traffic," I would say. "PR is for awareness." Back and forth, back and forth…. The net of this was that PR didn't drive much traffic and it was unlikely our target audience was reading many of the trade magazines so highly coveted by the PR team. However, what the placements and articles did provide for us was third-party validation in our solutions, which the sales team did use when talking with prospects. In addition, investors, board members, and strategic investors did watch and read these articles. While we continued to track traffic from PR sites, we didn't hold any illusions that PR was driving business for us. Our expenditure on it was correctly marked off as strategic, and allowed us to put the proper focus on this effort compared to other channels.

#6: Variety is Not the Spice of Marketing Metrics

Marketers love to do product bundles, or make different registration forms for some perceived need, or perhaps create a marketing program that is different from everything else ever done without any real reason or purpose beyond being different. While innovation and experimentation are part of marketing's DNA, there is a cost to implementing programs and processes that introduce variations into existing marketing processes.

If the standard for company web forms requires complete contact information, but marketing decides a particular white paper only requires name and email address, this seemingly simple change to a form could trigger multiple new process steps and hence requirements to measure success. Reducing form requirements is often done to see if reduced form requirements combined with more nurturing drive a higher overall level of qualified leads to sales. However, such a reduction in form information will distort other metrics unless this particular form is separated out from standard reporting.

Conversion rates, for example, will suddenly increase across the board due to the new form. Unless it is annotated somewhere, it can be forgotten in six months' time that the new form increased conversion rates. Email marketing campaigns may actually suffer when emailing these short-form prospects. Since these prospects had less of a commitment to the company in the first place, the follow-on email may be unwelcome. Since shorter forms may not contain sufficient information to route to sales, additional progressive profiling may be required to collect information for sales routing. This adds another process step that has to be measured and maintained.

Variety and experimentation are good things in marketing. But there is a cost associated with this variability that needs to be taken into consideration prior to implementing an experiment or a new program.

#7: Conservation of Metrics Property

With a full-blown measurement system in operation, the number of metrics tracked can grow to be unwieldy. But how do you know what should be tracked and what should not be tracked?

In general, once the baseline metrics are recorded, adding a new metric should only occur if it:

- Provides information that can be used to change or impact marketing tactics
- Requires consistent periodic review where historical comparisons are important
- Confirms proper system operation, and there is no existing way to validate that the system is operating correctly

While tracking marketing metrics, it's common for ideas to arise regarding new items worth tracking. Immediately, however, the question should be asked: "If we tracked that, what would we do with the information?" This follow-on question many times eliminates from consideration the addition of a new metric. If your company has no specific marketing programs targeted at India, then breaking out direct from organic traffic for India may be interesting, but it would not drive any behavior change in marketing since there are no programs associated with the country. In addition, the data could already be reconstructed since web analytics applications enable historical reviews of data at daily, weekly, or monthly time intervals.

The last point is especially true for all metrics. If a consistent review of a metric on a recurring basis is not useful and the data can be pulled from an existing system that includes this historical data, then pulling and recording the information may not serve any useful purpose. Weekly historical record of data from a particular website could be interesting to add to the metrics sheet, but that level of detail can be easily pulled if needed from the web analytics application. A more useful measure might be to understand total referring site traffic week over week, rather than a monthly comparison of traffic by site in order to pick up changes by major referring sites.

Metrics should be added to detect breakdowns in the lead generation process. Lead systems are complex operations that start with website traffic and end with sales opportunities. If not instrumented correctly, data fields, workflows, forms, and human process steps can all break and leave data, and hence prospects, stranded in the database. You could decide just to measure the number of new leads each day that show up for the sales team by examining what is in Salesforce.com. Doing this, however, leaves you blind to all the pieces of the system that must come together to get these leads into the system. Such pieces include a website that can be easily found as well as web forms, a marketing automation system, and a CRM system that are all working correctly. By measuring the amount of traffic to the site and the number of form completions, over time, the ratio of form completions to new leads can be established. A sudden change in this ratio indicates a problem or change somewhere in the process of how leads are captured, scored, and routed from the website to the sales team. Hence, any new program that introduces a different type of lead flow will require additional metrics to validate proper lead flow operation.

At some point, however, the number of metrics tracked will reach saturation. At this point, you have hit the point of conservation of metrics. The law of the conservation of metrics states that for every new metric added, one metric must be removed. Finding metrics to cut from tracking is not as difficult as it may seem if:

- The metric is not providing early warning to a failure of the system

- No discernible change has occurred in the metric and it is easily tracked by other mechanisms
- The metric produces data that is not actionable
- Little discussion occurs each week when the metric is referenced

If any of these three conditions are met, you have grounds for invoking the conservation of metrics rule and eliminating the collection and tracking of the metric. Removing such metrics is critical as the team hones in on the core metrics that drive the business.

#8: The Long Tail Takes Time

Weekly measurements for B2B marketers are important to understanding the operating tempo of the business and validating that the complex systems required to deliver leads from a website to a sales rep are operating correctly. Sometimes weekly numbers are so low as to be inconsequential or meaningless, except as a check that the system is operating correctly. But, over time, these smaller weekly results gradually build into monthly, then yearly, trends. Hitting the one-year point on a consistent set of measurements provides invaluable intelligence with not only significant history recorded, but the ability to compare similar months of performance year over year. Seasonal variations to traffic and visitors will occur due to holidays, events, product announcements, and other disruptions to what is normal traffic. For measurements of long tail items such as keywords, significant time may be required for any kind of trend to emerge in long tail data.

Hence the buildup of historical data over 12 months is highly valuable as a reference point for both the coming 12 months, and also as a backward look at long tail data values. It takes time for trends and values to emerge. Long tail tracking enables this to happen.

It is not guaranteed, however, that simply operating a site for an extended period of time will enable this data collection and valuable long tail data mining. Many changes to a company's go to market plan that seem innocent can significantly disrupt this long tail measurement. Projects that can have major impact on measurement and reporting include:

- Major website refreshes that change structure, URLs, and visitor flow
- Product name changes
- Dramatic changes to the home page
- Changes in pay-per-click strategies from quantity of traffic to quality of traffic, or vice versa
- Changes to the blog structure
- End of life for key products
- Website page clean-up that eliminates key referring site landing pages

While on their own each of these items may not be catastrophic, add them together and the comparison of today's traffic will be very different than similar traffic from the prior 12 months. For this reason, plans to make such changes for what may appear to be good reasons must be balanced against the potential loss of historical insight they may cause. New VPs of marketing commonly, for example, immediately embark on a website refresh, either for their own reasons or because the CEO has made the website change the VP's first job. Yet a website refresh can obliterate much of the historical information in the site. So rather than doing a refresh, unless the data collection and analysis have already been done, new execs would be better off measuring exactly how the site is performing across all dimensions to baseline operations prior to the refresh. Then, armed with this data, the refresh could be planned in order to improve specific areas of site operations. The reality is that once a metrics-oriented approach gets started, the concept of a complete site refresh generally goes out the window. A complete site refresh is a daunting task that almost never rises to the top of the work list when smaller, incremental changes have the ability to provide almost immediate site improvements. In metrics-driven organizations, it makes more sense to preserve the long tail and implement incremental improvements that drive real progress than to make sweeping changes that may not produce any measurable improvements.

#9: Getting Close Enough

Developing metrics is critical for understanding an organization's operation. At the same time, using limited sampling to establish rules of thumb for campaign performance, among other metrics, is not a bad process for limiting the amount of metric and data collection required. Sampling of metrics for campaigns allows for the quick creation of rules of thumb that can be used for decision making. Sampling also enables a reduction in metric tracking, especially for campaigns that tend to return the same results week over week.

Using sampling to reduce metric tracking can be especially effective when the velocity of new campaigns is very high. Ideally, most campaigns go through a formal process to evaluate their effectiveness several weeks, then months, after the campaign concludes. However in volume marketing models, the pace of program roll-out may be very rapid. Nurturing programs, for example, may change weekly. While attempting to measure the success of each nurture email to generate opportunities may be interesting, it could also be overwhelming and may not necessarily provide actionable information.

A better approach for high-volume programs that have significant variability is to sample campaign success for a period of time. If a particular campaign with a particular type of offer was successful in March, repeating the program in August against a similar sample size should yield similar results. For example, if history shows that email campaigns with particular content offers result in leads that have a 10% opportunity creation rate, tracking this opportunity creation rate for a similar campaign repeated six months later may not be necessary. Rather, provided the click-through rates and form conversion rates are similar for each new campaign that runs with a similar offer, one could assume the opportunity conversion rates would be the same.

But even without this intense measurement at the campaign level, since weekly metrics most likely look at opportunity creation rate at the aggregate level across all campaigns, a noticeable drop or lack of increase in this total opportunity creation rate may be enough to trigger further investigation should the campaign fail. Most marketing teams get very tuned in to what works and what results to expect given the programs run the prior week. If the 10%

opportunity creation rate program run six months prior didn't cause opportunity creation numbers to increase, the team will recognize this and investigate even without tracking the specific results for this campaign weekly.

#10: Low Sample Sizes Can Lead to Wrong Conclusions

Many times marketing organizations base conclusions on the success of a program based on a very small sample size of responses. One opportunity created on 20 responses is theoretically a 10% opportunity creation rate. But the sample size is so small that there is no way to confidently move forward under the assumption that getting 200 responses from the same program would yield similar results. Understanding the minimum required sample size from a marketing program to get either 95% or 99% confidence requires a combination of both art and math. But making definitive judgments based on low sample size results can lead to the wrong conclusion.

#11: SLAs = Relationship Failure

Many organizations use the term SLA or "service level agreement" to spell out the time frame in which sales is supposed to follow up on leads. The use of this term just sets the stage for antagonism between sales and marketing. Sales is not delivering a service to marketing that requires an SLA. The reality is that if you ask sales managers how soon after reps are given hot leads should they follow up, most will say immediately. Everyone, most of all the sales team, wants to generate revenue since their paycheck is dependent on it. Sales organizations understand that leads sitting untouched lose value hourly. Yet, for some reason, there exists the need to set up an SLA between sales and marketing. This is the wrong approach. The sales leadership owns keeping their people focused on lead follow-up. This doesn't mean that sales should not set a lead follow-up time. Sales needs to set this follow-up time and measure against it so leads go through a consistent process, allowing programs to be measured against each other with as many controlled conditions as possible. Lead follow-up time is one of those controlled conditions. A program that gets immediate results compared to a program in which the reps follow up weeks later is likely to get dramatically better sales results, regardless of the quality of the latter program. The key here, and much of this is semantics, is that SLAs create the wrong relationship and imply the wrong ownership to lead follow-up. The sales team owns lead follow-up times. They need to declare the values and measure their team against them.

#12: Curiosity Killers: Dashboards and Centralized Analysis Teams

In Chapter 11 we discussed the organizational structure for a metrics-driven organization. A key to making such an organization work is to empower everyone with access to the metrics and numbers they need to do their jobs. A centralized analysis team that considers the use, access, and publication of metrics as their domain may fight against such a trend. On the surface, it seems to make sense to centralize analysis so that there is one set of truth. But by ceding this control and, more importantly, knowledge of how to get data, marketing teams lose some major capabilities that are critical to their success.

First, by moving marketing analytics and analysis to a central team and away from the individual person responsible for delivering a result, the analysis part becomes the job of someone else. Accountability for reporting the numbers is now the job of a different person. If the numbers are low, or high, or not believable, the person accountable for the numbers can rightfully question the source. This questioning process introduces delay, doubt, and uncertainty into the rapid-fire metrics process. By keeping those responsible for the numbers also responsible for analyzing and pulling those numbers, the chain of provenance of metrics is preserved.

Second, centralized analysis teams rob the front-line marketers of the ability to question, explore, and gain new insight from the data they see each week. The weekly or monthly metrics represent what is important to run the business. But behind these metrics should lie a deeper understanding of what is happening to deliver the numbers. This deeper understanding only comes about if everyone on the team can drill down, question, and be intellectually curious about the data they see. If this curiosity requires them to submit requests to a central data team, wait a week, then see if the team answered their questions, their curiosity will be killed. Everyone on the marketing team needs to be intellectually curious about what is happening with the data and be enabled to follow their curiosity to get deeper answers.

The close cousin of centralized analysis systems are centralized dashboards. CMOs and others always want dashboards to run the business. But dashboards are only effective if they represent a summation of knowledge that everyone has, as opposed to a simplification of information where no one understands the source. A dashboard showing total website traffic, for example, only makes sense if everyone understands the component parts of the total traffic number and can drill down to see these numbers. Even then, a traffic dashboard only makes sense if everyone can drill down even further to the source data to verify that the referring site traffic, for example, is really referring site traffic and not some misplaced paid campaign. Without providing the ability to get to source data, dashboards lose their value. Dashboards are a valuable way to display information, but they should present a selection of the best of all the metrics the team already understands, rather than the only metrics they will see.

#13: Avoid the Peanut Butter Effect

Many marketing teams with lots of products will attempt to go to market on a per-product basis and will divide marketing resources among all the products. This spreading of scarce marketing resources too thinly results in large operational inefficiencies. Ten unique Google AdWords programs focused on ten different products and users, each spending $1,000 per month, is such a thin spend that it will be very difficult to get sufficient information or metrics to determine what is working. Worse, the operational overhead to run all ten programs will be very high. Taking that same $10,000 per month and putting it behind one or two products will decrease administrative overhead and get substantial results that the AdWords program can use to tune and improve effectiveness.

Organizations many times want marketing to market as many products as possible. But in the real-time, operationally focused marketing world, each product needs to have sufficient resources to succeed. Peanut butter spreading of resources is a recipe for inefficiency and poor results.

#14: Metrics without Owners are Like Stray Dogs

This book contains all kinds of metrics to be measured. But if a metric is to be measured, it has to have an owner who can report on the metric and drive or work to change its outcomes. Otherwise, a metric without an owner quickly loses relevance and is lost. When a metric is reported as being out of specification but no one is responsible for it, the fact it is out of specification is irrelevant. There is no one to take action, fix it, and report back. Worse, metrics without owners can be challenged as to the validity of their data if there is no one standing behind them to say "That data is correct, I pulled it." Metrics need owners.

#15: Breaking the Metrics Problem into Smaller Parts

While all metrics need owners, the best metrics get subdivided into smaller and smaller component parts. The CMO, theoretically, is responsible for all traffic. But if you report on just total traffic, the CMO has no one to delegate the task of increasing traffic. Only by subdividing traffic by source can the CMO then delegate responsibility for increasing traffic to people who can actually impact the sum of all the parts. Metrics should be divided down until all the source components sit with front-line marketers who can influence their own parts of the problem.

#16: The Time to Get Results Exceeds the Patience of the CEO and VP of Sales – or – Give This Book to Your CEO for Christmas

Sales VPs and CEOs want results and they want results quickly. Of all the levers that can be pulled to drive results, few of them can be pulled quickly. Most take a long time, as in several quarters, to work. Even pay-per-click advertising could take several quarters to double or triple spending as the right words and programs and locations are discovered. The problem is that sales is driven quarterly. If the CMO is lucky enough to have been building the processes and procedures from the beginning and can keep up with the sales revenue ramp, then there should not be any problem. But a new CMO walking into a company that needs to grow without these types of programs in place will need several quarters at least for the marketing systems to start to scale. Setting expectations is therefore key.

Expectations alone won't be enough. The VP of sales and the CEO need to be educated on the complexities of the marketing process. In fact, some sales VPs are very curious about online marketing. CMOs need to spend significant time educating and discussing what they are doing and why and showing progress. Many marketing organizations lack visibility into what is happening and why. Marketing appears as a black hole through which leads appear, but most people don't know why. Provided you are comfortable with the management team, disclosing and educating on how the process works — including walking fellow executives through the operations — will go a long way at gaining appreciation for the time it takes to build a properly functioning team. This appreciation will also translate into a competitive advantage for the company as once it is built, it is difficult to replicate.

#17: Beware the Absolutes

There are very few marketing specifications that are absolute measures. In other words, if a metric is out of specification, catastrophic harm can happen to the organization or company. Even measures such as the time for sales to follow up on new leads, while important, are not necessarily critical. It is not catastrophic if a sales rep follows up 48 hours after a lead is presented to him instead of within 24 hours. Such follow-up is not ideal as the opportunity creation rate will be lower, but a ton of other factors could influence the success of that lead more than the follow-up time frame.

Avoiding absolutes is important and absolute measurements should be reserved for only the most critical measures. Making the lead follow-up time frame an absolute, for example, would require significant effort to ensure compliance within the sales team. In addition, in the face of too much compliance enforcement, reps will move leads to "follow-up" status with minimal effort simply to be compliant. Peer pressure, management pressure, and the reps' own observations of performance all represent better ways to drive compliance.

Key Boat Philosophy #1 – Pay Attention to Signs

In general on the boat, there were a lot of red signs you really had to pay attention to. Some red signs said things like "Do Not Enter, Deadly Force Authorized" which meant if you crossed the line, you could be shot. Another favorite, "High Radiation", was posted on the reactor compartment door. But there was one red sign that you really, really, really had to pay attention to.

Submarines in the '80s emptied their sewage tanks by coming up shallow, pressurizing their toilet system, and discharging overboard. The pressure was required since even coming up shallow, the submarine was still 50+ feet beneath the surface.

Prior to blowing sanitaries, red signs would be placed on all head doors saying "Blowing Sanitaries" so no one operated the toilet and vented the pressurized sewage tank into the submarine, rather than overboard. Besides being unpleasant for the poor soul operating the toilet who received a shower of the worst kind, venting the head in board would make the entire boat smell awful and the victim would be despised by all for stinking the boat up.

This inboard venting rarely happened, unless you were my stateroom mate, and you woke up in the middle of the night and had to use the head, and you had bad eyesight and you didn't put your contacts in, and the red sign didn't stand out much since the boat's nighttime interior lighting was red. My stateroom mate didn't make that mistake again.

Take Action

Setting up a metrics-driven organization, establishing an operating cadence, and following the philosophical points presented above should put a marketing team on the path to success. But what does success look like? What are the signs of success? In the next chapter we will examine the signs of success for a metrics-driven marketing team. But first, here is how you can take action:

- Review these philosophy points with your team, three per week for the next six weeks.
- Does your team agree? Disagree? What does sales think?
- Develop your own philosophy statements to help guide the organization.

Chapter 14: Signs of Success

What You Will Learn

- Success may be tough to detect with numbers
- Success starts to look more like the ability to know what is going on, make corrections, and steer in the right direction
- Success almost feels cultural
- Numbers must follow, but signs of success will be present long before the numbers prove it out

Overview

Up to this point, this book has provided a cookbook of how to build and operate a B2B metrics-driven organization. But how do you know when the team is successful? Certainly hitting lead generation and revenue goals is one indication, but that may not necessarily be the right indicator as marketing is only one part of the revenue generation process. A product with a bad market reputation will make it more difficult to generate leads. A sales team that is understaffed will find it difficult to make revenue goals. So while evaluating the team's effectiveness on numbers achievement may sound logical, it can lead a CEO or CMO astray.

A marketing team in a hot market with an excellent sales team and tremendous products can look like all-stars even though their contributions to the revenue effort are less than stellar. Conversely, a highly functional team trying to market poor products with an ineffective sales team can look like the cause of the problem. Praising a team operating at a poor level of execution just because the revenue results are good is no better than firing a CMO just because revenue numbers are bad.

To really determine how successfully a team is operating, therefore, requires a deeper look into marketing operations at both soft and numerical indicators of success. Firing a high-performance marketing team that is hampered by poor products or poor sales execution is just as bad as retaining a poor-performing team being kept afloat by great sales execution and products. Diagnosing correctly how the team is really performing is critical to making the right decisions.

The following sections outline some indicators of marketing success beyond the key metrics.

Fierce Devotion to Numbers and Goals

Regardless of whether a marketing team is hitting the goals, are they fiercely dedicated to them? Do they know the numbers and obsess over them? Does a great week of numbers put a bounce in everyone's step while a bad week makes people consider changing programs? If there is a Monday morning metrics review meeting, can you walk into the room without looking at the results and see who is happy or disappointed in last week's results based on nothing more than facial expressions? Is the atmosphere of hitting goals, missing goals, but always trying to win and learn contagious to the team? These are signs of an energized team trying to make the numbers regardless of obstacles placed in their way.

Learning Organization

A high-performance marketing team spends their time together in limited meetings learning from each other. If the team is operating correctly, the SEO person will want to know what is working with email marketing just as much as the product marketer will want to understand what pay-per-click programs are working. Keepers of the brand will understand why some PPC words work better than others and can give feedback on why a particular ad campaign is good or bad. Brand people will really get the persona of the target customer and can provide guidance to all on how to drive more conversions and clicks. Members of a properly operating team is constantly learning from each other as each person delivers their numbers for their areas of responsibility. They realize they have to learn from each other since their success depends on leveraging each other's learnings in order to deliver results.

This constant sharing of information and ideas also enables an informal cross-training. Done correctly over a long enough period of time, marketers doing one function, say SEO, could easily transition to running the nurturing campaigns and operations. Moves and shifts on the team are possible as everyone has been around the other marketing levers enough to allow for easy transitions. While the ability to transition is good, this ability is also representative of the team's interdependent nature, which is a good indicator of success.

Creative Destruction of Metrics

With metrics the foundation for marketing effectiveness, an effective team starts to challenge, develop, and come up with new ways to look at metrics and analysis. High-functioning teams object to metrics that provide them no value, and seek out new ways to measure programs to improve effectiveness. New measures aren't seen as a burden but rather a chance to improve results via deeper understandings of the marketing process. The thirst for data and understanding permeates the team as they try to crack the code on what is working and what is not working.

Numbers-Driven Decision Making

Much like everyone believes they can sell products, many people in an organization believe they have the next best marketing idea to drive lots of revenue for the company. Sometimes these ideas from outside the marketing team can pay off or at least cause marketing to look at a problem differently and come up with a superior answer. The manner in which the marketing team analyzes new ideas generated both within and outside the marketing group is a good indicator of how well marketing understands the operational flow of prospects as they move through the buying cycle.

A metrics-driven marketing team will respond to a request to run marketing programs from sales, for example, with a balanced metrics-oriented answer as to why a particular program could or could not be run, and what types of numerical requirements would be required from sales to make a program meet potential ROI hurdles. Sales teams many times will want to attend physical events for a variety of reasons. If the marketing team responds with answers such as "That show is no good" or "The leads were bad last year", these answers reveal a team that is not up on the operational flows and results from trade show execution. As a sales manager, answers like this would only make me question marketing's decisions even more. But if the team responds to sales with, "We can do that, but it's a lightly attended event, so you will need to get 40% of all event attendees by the booth to make it work. Can you do that?", a constructive dialogue can start on how to make an event successful.

Marketing decisions should be numerically driven, not subjective. Highly functional teams get this.

Decision Making is Pushed Down to the Lowest Organizational Level

In a metrics-driven marketing organization, decisions can be made by front-line marketers since decisions are based on objective analysis of yields rather than the subjective opinions of senior management on what works or does not work. In the prior example of the trade show, if the sales team doesn't think they can capture 40% of the show attendees, then the event will have a poor ROI compared to other programs. No head of sales or marketing would push to attend such an event unless there was some strategic reason for attendance. This decision can be made low in the organization, however, because the decision maker has statistical analysis to back up the decision. Even if sales wanted to escalate the issue with sales leadership, the sales leadership team also understands the challenges of yield and cost per lead since they are engaged with the marketing team. The escalation wouldn't go anywhere because both teams understand the numbers.

Shifting Assessment of Program Effectiveness is Called Out

How many times have you been on a marketing call and heard someone report that an event or program was "good" or "generated awareness" or there was "lots of activity"? These measures of success are subjective and essentially meaningless. Without some numerical measurement, it is impossible to tell if a program operated well or not.

In a similar manner, shifting metrics of assessment should also be greeted with skepticism from a high-performance team. If one week referring site traffic is reported as a percentage increase over the week before, then the following week the number is presented as an absolute value, that should provoke howls of complaints from the team. Metrics need to be reported in absolute terms followed by some measure of whether the absolute value represents growth, shrinkage, or some other measure of change over prior reporting periods. Keeping everyone honest in their analysis of key metrics is a sign of a high-performance team.

Back-of-the-Envelope Factoids

A high-performance marketing organization starts to really understand the metrics and numbers to move prospects from left to right in the sales funnel. Over time, the team will develop a solid back-of-the-envelope memory of various marketing statistics that can make the decision-making process on new programs go quickly. These statistics could involve:

- Cost per sales-qualified lead from paid programs
- Average click-through rates for email marketing
- Website conversion rates
- Percentage of site traffic by source
- Average bounce rates
- Number of badge swipes expected given trade show attendance numbers
- Number of webinar attendees based on registration
- Cost of all pay-per-lead programs and expected opportunity yield
- Sales opportunity creation numbers based on lead source
- Overall sales opportunity creation numbers

High-performance marketing teams know their numbers and know the key metrics that drive decision making. Memorizing the key metrics that drive the business enables accelerated decision making and rapid analysis of results.

Parallel Communication and Decision Making

In a high-performance marketing organization, most of the communication and work occurs between the marketers responsible for driving their own specific traffic areas, not up and down with the manager. Since everyone generally has the same goals of pushing traffic and conversions but with different techniques, the team members are incented to communicate and share knowledge with each other. In fact, without this, the team will fail. Hence the marketing leader doesn't add as much value to a team member as their peers do. While the marketing leader can coordinate, coach, and help drive the discussion, the team really works when the team members are driving the business themselves. A successful email marketing campaign, for example, may be seized upon by the PPC team member to revise keywords while the SEO team member may decide to build some pages based on the knowledge gained from the mailing. Conversely, some high traffic to some new keywords may trigger the content marketer to develop a new white paper that the email marketing person is able to use in an upcoming nurture mailing.

If the team is operating in this high-performance manner, meetings get held without the team leader to discuss and plan upcoming programs. When the team does come together to walk through upcoming plans, it is as though they have already met, which in most cases they will have since team members must coordinate and work together to succeed. For a high-performance team, metrics meetings are less about team members reporting to the leader, and more about team members seeing if there is anything in the other person's data that can help them with their own efforts. High-performance marketing teams are fun to be on, slightly stressful due to the intensity of work, but highly rewarding from both a learning and career standpoint.

Uncomfortable Programs that Make CMOs Squeamish

Of course if the marketing team does meet the criteria as a high-performance team, it also means you have a rabble of marketers who work closely together, have strong opinions on what will work, and understand the details of their particular areas in an order of magnitude better than the manager. The result is that the CIO or team leader is going to be presented with programs and ideas that may appear destined for failure, or just plain whacky. To squash these ideas is not a good practice since it destroys the team's initiative and, more importantly, could destroy programs and ideas that have extremely high potential ROI. By pushing decision making and discussion down into the organization, the team becomes extremely innovative since ideas don't get tempered by senior management or the constant concern that "the CIO will never approve this." It is hypocritical on one hand to goal a marketing team on hitting specific numbers, but then disapprove well-thought-out programs designed to help them hit those numbers.

A large part of developing these teams requires that the CIO or other senior marketing leader has to feel comfortable in gradually letting go of much of the marketing activity. This delegation process also has to extend to the CEO. Nothing will crush the initiative of a marketing team faster if they know the CEO has to approve every marketing-oriented idea. In fact, marketers will quickly realize they are set up to fail if, on one hand, they are asked to produce results, but on the other hand they are not given the latitude to achieve them.

This is, of course, a tricky balancing act. The CMO has to be concerned about the corporate brand, among other items. But if the company leadership hires star marketers, they need to trust them to execute. Eventually, they will. This leads to the next point: celebrating failure.

Celebrating Failure

Not everything the marketing team proposes will work well. To some extent, there is a sliding scale of success from completely terrible to wildly successful that is the difference between 0% response and 15% response. The key is to celebrate the failures, learn from them, and enshrine them in the marketing team's memory so mistakes are not repeated. And if a similar tactic is tried in the future, everyone must be made aware of the difference between the old tactic that failed and the new tactic with a twist.

Most initial marketing attempts will actually fail and produce poor results. But over time and with repetition and refinement, results will gradually improve. A requirement that all marketing must succeed on the first attempt stifles innovation, pushes teams to try only the most conservative approaches, and effectively caps the high end of success for what is considered a truly great program. Greatness in marketing execution only happens with constant repetition, failure, correction, improvement, and experimentation. If the culture does not support the celebration of failure, this cycle of success will never happen.

Take Action

Firing a high-performance marketing team due to poor product or sales execution can be as catastrophic as keeping a low-performing team due to perceived success caused by excellence in product and sales execution. When evaluating a team, the key is to look at both numbers and results plus the culture of the team in order to access overall performance. CEOs who fail to analyze marketing's effectiveness in this way often misdiagnose revenue misses, assign the blame to marketing, then spend a year hiring a new CMO and waiting for results that may never come if the problem in revenue generation actually lies elsewhere. Marketing measurement once again appears as both art and science. Next steps:

- Evaluate your team with this success criteria in mind.
- How far off are you from this definition of success?
- Can you become successful with your current team or team structure?

Chapter 15: Conclusion

You made it to the end! Hopefully the magnitude of metrics presented in this book didn't scare you off. The key is not so much the specific metrics, but creating a culture that uses metrics to verify operations, drive behavior of individuals, and make high-level decisions. The complexity of today's marketing organizations requires this level of analysis. I firmly believe that marketers who learn this operational aspect of marketing will be the marketers sought out by employers as the next generation of CMOs.

Much of what was covered in this book represents a snapshot of marketing operations in 2014. Parts of the book may already be out of date, but the concepts are not. To drive revenue, you need leads. To get leads, you need traffic that converts. To get traffic, you need compelling content and paid programs that work. To get traffic to convert, you need a site that works and offers that make sense. To get leads from these conversions, you need to nurture prospects. To get revenue from leads, you need to enable a sales team and monitor the flow of leads as they become opportunities. This is all very basic blocking and tackling, until you start to look at the volume of leads and the traffic required to build a substantial business. Without a maniacal focus on traffic numbers and on growing these numbers, a business would have to be very lucky to achieve the scale required to succeed.

Marketing operations is only going to grow as a key requirement for CMOs to be successful. You can get started tomorrow by capturing just a few key metrics each week. Once started, these few metrics will create "the ask" for more metrics and you will be on your way to a metrics-driven organization. But you have to take the first step with the first group of metrics. Start today, and in six months you will have begun to understand how marketing is operating in an order of magnitude greater than any you have ever seen.

APPENDIX A: Metrics

You can download the metrics mentioned in this book from www.storymetrix.com/resources.

Made in the USA
San Bernardino, CA
16 April 2015